THE KETO
One
FOR
COOKBOOK

100 Delicious Make-Ahead, Make-Fast Meals for One (OR TWO) That Make Low-Carb Simple and Easy

DANA CARPENDER

Best-selling author of *500 Paleo Recipes* and *500 Ketogenic Recipes*

FAIR WINDS

Brimming with creative inspiration, how-to projects, and useful information to enrich your everyday life, Quarto Knows is a favorite destination for those pursuing their interests and passions. Visit our site and dig deeper with our books into your area of interest: Quarto Creates, Quarto Cooks, Quarto Homes, Quarto Lives, Quarto Drives, Quarto Explores, Quarto Gifts, or Quarto Kids.

First Published in 2019 by Fair Winds Press, an imprint of The Quarto Group,
100 Cummings Center, Suite 265-D, Beverly, MA 01915, USA.
T (978) 282-9590 F (978) 283-2742 QuartoKnows.com

Fair Winds Press titles are also available at discount for retail, wholesale, promotional, and bulk purchase. For details, contact the Special Sales Manager by email at specialsales@quarto.com or by mail at The Quarto Group, Attn: Special Sales Manager, 100 Cummings Center, Suite 265-D, Beverly, MA 01915, USA.

23 22 21 20 19   1 2 3 4 5

ISBN: 978-1-59233-868-9

Digital edition published in 2019
eISBN: 978-1-63159-679-7

Library of Congress Cataloging-in-Publication Data is available.

Cover Images: Alison Bickel Photography
Design and Page Layout: Sporto
Photography: Alison Bickel Photography

Printed in China

MIX
Paper from
responsible sources
FSC® C008047

DEDICATION

To all the doctors and researchers, from William Harvey, MD, who famously put an obese undertaker named William Banting on a carbohydrate-restricted diet with historic success, to Vilhjalmur Stefansson, the polar explorer who lived in the Bellevue Hospital Dietetic Ward for a year to prove that an "Eskimo diet" of nothing but fatty meat would yield good health.

To Rollin Woodyatt, MD, who first identified ketone bodies in fasting epileptics and realized they were what was quelling the seizures. To Alan Kekwick, professor of medicine; Gaston Pawan, research biochemist; and later Stephen Benoit, MD, whose work demonstrated that altering macronutrient ratios yielded changes in metabolism. To John Yudkin, MD, whose insistence that sugar, not fat, was the cause of heart disease cost him his career, and to Robert Atkins, MD, who simply laughed at his many critics and said, "Someday they'll catch up to me."

To modern pioneers of ketogenic diet research such as Eric Westman, MD, whose work at Duke University has led to his diabetic patients routinely achieving normal blood sugar with no medication, and Richard Bernstein, MD, whose extensive knowledge and understanding of ketogenic diets for diabetes was won the hard way, starting with treating his own Type I diabetes.

To Professor Richard Feinman and Dr. Eugene Fine who have demonstrated the value of a ketogenic diet for cancer treatment. To Stephen Phinney, MD, PhD, and Jeff Volek, PhD, RD, who have demonstrated that a ketogenic diet can improve athletic endurance. To Stephen Cunnane, PhD, and Russell H. Swerdlow, MD, who are investigating the power of a ketogenic diet to fight the tragedy of dementia.

In short, to everyone who was and is curious, wise, brave, and honest enough to buck the system, to examine the evidence instead going with the accepted wisdom, and to share their knowledge with the world, the critics be damned.

CONTENTS

WHAT IS A KETO DIET?

Wow. After a couple of decades of being told that being in ketosis was dangerous, nutritional ketosis is finally being recognized as the widely beneficial health intervention it is. It's about time. So, let's start with a basic but important question:

WHAT IS A KETO DIET?

Oh boy, there are a lot of, uh, interesting assertions about this out there. So let me clarify: A ketogenic diet is any diet that is low enough in carbohydrates that your body is forced to shift over to burning fat as its main source of fuel. Ketones are a natural by-product of fat-burning and can be used as fuel by most tissues that cannot burn free fatty acids, allowing the combination of fat and ketones to provide almost all—but not quite all—of your body's fuel. Any diet that forces your body into fat-burning—and therefore ketone-producing—mode is a ketogenic diet. Period.

I state this because I hear people saying things like, "Oh, it's like a low-carb diet, only you eat only *clean* foods, no chemicals or artificial sweeteners!" or "You have to eat 20 grams a day or less of carbohydrates, and at least 80 percent of your calories from fat," or "You have to be careful not to eat too much protein." All of those are possibly valuable guidelines, but they are not essential to a ketogenic diet.

ABOUT FAT

Ketogenic diets were first devised to mimic the effects of fasting for treating epileptic seizures. When a person fasts, they tap into their body fat for fuel. That fat-burning creates ketones, which in turn fuel those tissues that cannot burn free fatty acids, especially the brain. This is why our hunter-gatherer ancestors didn't curl up into fuzzy-headed blobs and starve to death when they ran short of food—they could run off body fat efficiently enough to go hunt and gather.

A ketogenic diet, by cutting carbohydrates, and therefore glucose, to a bare minimum, forces fat burning. But be aware of a few caveats.

Testing positive for ketosis proves that you are running a fat-burning metabolism. However, it says nothing about the *source of that fat*. You could be burning body fat, sure, but you could also be burning dietary fat, the fat from your last meal. You simply do not, cannot, know.

A ketogenic diet will be a high-fat diet, but how high in fat? To some degree, that will depend on your purpose for eating keto. If you're eating keto for improved brain health—a great idea—then it doesn't matter whether you're burning body fat or dietary fat. The same goes for keto-adapted endurance athletes. But if you're eating a keto diet to lose weight, the most common purpose, it matters.

I point this out because fat bombs, butter- and oil-laced coffee, and other very concentrated sources of fat, have become popular in the keto world. I've used them myself, especially when fat fasting (eating 1000 calories per day, as close to 90 percent of them from fat as possible). These can provide energy and quell hunger, which is great. But if you overconsume them, your body may very well never bother to tap into its fat stores. In other words: One cup of butter and coconut oil–laced coffee, such as Bulletproof Coffee, can get you going in the morning and suppress hunger for much of the day, but drinking it all day may well prevent weight loss (and could make you jumpy, too).

Yes, this is Calories In, Calories Out, but a ketogenic diet changes the math. In their landmark 1956 clinical trial published in *The Lancet*, researchers Kekwick and Pawan demonstrated that a very low-carbohydrate diet lets people eat more calories than they could on a "mixed" or "balanced" diet—roughly 600 calories more per day—and still lose weight. This allows weight loss without hunger. That's a real advantage, especially when coupled with the appetite suppression of ketosis. But, of course, there are individual differences in metabolisms, which cause people to respond differently to the same diets.

What this means is that stating that a ketogenic diet must provide X percent of its calories from fat is too broad. *If you want to lose weight, some of the fat that is burned must come from your own fat stores.*

I'm unconvinced that being in a very deep state of ketosis is essential for weight loss, although it is needed for some therapeutic purposes, such as seizure control and combating dementia. So as long as you're testing in at least a mild-to-moderate state of ketosis, you know you're burning fat for fuel.

Ketosis can be tested by urine strips, blood ketone meters (similar to, and often combined with, blood glucose meters), or breath meters. Urine strips are cheapest and most widely available, but least accurate. Blood testing is the gold standard, but involves finger-sticks and it's pricey—the test strips run about $5 each. Breath meters are reasonably accurate and coming down in price. I use a breath meter, but it only tells me "mild/moderate/deep" ketosis (or none at all, but that hasn't happened).

SO HOW DO I KNOW HOW MUCH FAT TO EAT?

By paying attention to your protein and carb intake, you will know how much fat to eat. If that sounds backward, let me explain.

Protein is essential for repair and maintenance of the body. *How much* protein is essential is another point of contention. I have heard cogent arguments made for eating no more than 1 gram of protein per kilo (or roughly 2 pounds) of healthy body weight. I have heard equally cogent arguments that as much as 2 grams of protein per kilo, or a gram per pound, of healthy body weight is better. Again, this will be individual and will vary with your genetics and how active you are, how good your liver is at converting amino acids to glucose, and possibly some other things I'm not thinking of.

So, start with your healthy body weight—not the weight that would make you fashionably ultra thin, just a healthy weight for your height and bone structure. If that's 120 pounds, then you should eat no fewer than 60 grams of protein per day, and not much more than 120 grams. Whether you do well toward the lower or higher end of that range is something you can only learn through trial and error.

Then figure your carb intake: 20 grams per day is a pretty common goal, though some people can stay in ketosis with as much as 50 grams per day, while others have to drop as low as 10 grams per day.

Both protein and carbohydrates have 4 calories per gram. If you're at the low end of this range, eating 60 grams of protein and 20 grams of carb, you will be getting 320 calories from protein and carbs. If you eat about 1800 calories per day total, you need to consume another 1480 calories from fat. Divide 1480 by 1800 and that tells you that 82 percent of your calories should come from fat. Fat has 9 calories per gram, so it'll take about 165 grams of fat to supply the rest of your calories.

On the other hand, if you eat 120 grams of protein and 50 grams of carbohydrate per day, you are getting 680 calories from protein and carbs. Again assuming 1800 calories per day, you are left with 1120 calories to add from fat, or 124 grams. In this case, you'd be eating 62 percent of your calories from fat. Would you be in ketosis? That's a question for test strips or a breath ketone meter. Would you feel as well? That's a question for your own body. There's no substitute for paying attention.

STRAIGHT CARNIVORY

There is a growing subset of the keto movement that embraces straight carnivory—eating nothing but meat, usually fatty meat such as rib-eye steaks, pork shoulder, bacon, and ground beef; some also eat eggs. I have not tried this; I like cooking and enjoying a variety of food too much, but I know people who are ecstatic about the results they are getting, in terms of both weight and health. Many combine straight carnivory with intermittent fasting, eating, say, a big steak and some bacon just once a day. If you dislike meal planning and cooking, there are worse ideas.

That said, while such a diet offers just about zero carb, it doesn't generally hit the 80 percent of calories from fat mark. Even fatty meat generally runs in the low 70 percent range. Again, that's where burning body fat comes in.

TOTAL OR NET CARBS?

There has been a strong move back to counting total carbs. Given how the food processing industry abused the concept of net carbs, this makes sense. Declaring everything from maltitol and fructose as resistant starch that doesn't "count" was and is sheer marketing nonsense.

But I find the net carb concept, originally devised by Drs. Michael and Mary Dan Eades under the term "effective carb count," to be reasonable: They advocated subtracting fiber *and only fiber* from the total carb count, because the human gut cannot digest or absorb fiber. This originally was meant to allow people to eat a few more non-starchy vegetables and low-sugar fruits, not cookies, candy, and bread. And, truth to tell, I often see both advocates of net carbs and of total carbs eating non-starchy vegetables fairly freely. It's not the lettuce you need to be wary of, it's the possible sugar in the dressing.

Many people are not aware of the carb counts of seasonings, such as herbs and spices, most of which run 1 to 2 grams of carbohydrate per teaspoon, although, again, some of that comes from fiber.

You can count total or net carbs; I've provided both. But unless you're very sensitive, an extra gram or two by way of a little curry powder or an extra ¼ cup of cauliflower isn't likely to do much harm.

And as you'll read later on, I discount one other carb: erythritol, the only sugar alcohol (polyol) that passes through the human body completely unabsorbed.

CHAPTER 1

KETO COOKING FOR ONE (OR TWO)

I have never focused much on small-batch recipes, keto or otherwise. Some things, like omelets or chops, automatically come in single-serving sizes. But my husband and I are not averse to leftovers around here; I've never bothered trying to make, say, chili or meatloaf in small batches. Some things, such as pot roast, defy single-serving batches, while others, like baked custard, are just too much time and trouble to bother with single-serving batches.

So working on this book, I came to a new realization: Some things are made in big batches because that's the way the ingredients are packaged. You can buy a head of cabbage—heck, my grocery store offers half-heads—or a bag of coleslaw mix, but either one is going to make a lot more than one or two servings of slaw. If you're like me and will happily eat slaw on the side with every darned thing for four days straight, this will work out for you. On the other hand, if you want slaw now, but not tomorrow and Wednesday, you're going to have leftover cabbage, which means either making another cabbage dish within a few

days, or having leftover cabbage age into a swampy microclimate in your refrigerator—and if you let the rest of an ingredient go bad, you've wasted money. Same thing with a 1-pound (445 g) package of ground beef, an 8-ounce (225 g) container of mushrooms, a bag of fresh cauli-rice, and so on.

I have made some assumptions about the keto single, chief among them that you are busy and want your recipes to be fairly quick and easy. I also assume that you would prefer not to heat up your oven if you can avoid it—it just seems silly to me to spend the time and the energy to heat up the oven for one serving. Accordingly, most of these recipes call for stove-top cooking, and especially for skillet-cooking. I have only used the oven when I couldn't work out a quicker and easier method of cooking.

Speaking of skillets: If you haven't tried the new ceramic nonstick skillets, you should. I recommend them highly, especially for eggs. A 7-inch to 8-inch ceramic nonstick skillet with a good heavy bottom will serve you endlessly.

Here are some strategies I've hit on in writing this book that will help you, too:

- *Find a grocery store with a good salad bar.* This allows you to buy just a cup (235 ml) of cauliflower, baby spinach, broccoli, sliced mushrooms; a tablespoon's worth of shredded carrot, enough sliced onion to make a tablespoon or two minced, a half dozen cherry tomatoes—in short, just what you need.

- *Look for a grocery or specialty food store with a Mediterranean bar*, one with a wide array of olives, marinated feta, marinated mushrooms, bocconcini (little balls of marinated high-quality mozzarella), roasted red peppers—all kinds of stuff that fits a keto plan. I have fallen in love with a blend of feta in ¼-inch (6 mm) dice, stuffed green olives, and kalamata olives, all marinated together in olive oil and spices. Useful in so many ways!

- *Look for vegetables you can buy in small quantity.* Does your grocery store carry cut-up cauliflower and broccoli that lets you buy only as much as you like? Can you buy a small tub of celery sticks so you don't have to buy a whole head of the stuff? (Sadly, my nearest salad bar lacks diced celery.)

- *Buy a jar of minced garlic.* Why? Because single-serving recipes often need only a half clove, leaving you with the other half. With jarred minced garlic you can simply use ¼ teaspoon.

- *Stock up on plain frozen vegetables.* (Skip the ones with sauces and other carb-laden additives.) You will be able to keep a few varieties in the house, use only what you need, and stash the rest for later. I was a very happy girl when I discovered my Aldi carries frozen cauli-rice, having had some fresh cauli-rice rot on me. Frozen pureed cauliflower, affectionately known to keto dieters as "fauxtatoes," is now widely available, and makes more sense for the keto single than making it fresh.

- *Buy little vegetables.* I've been buying bags of "baby" cucumbers; one sliced baby cuke makes about ½ cup (120 ml). I've also discovered Campari tomatoes, vine tomatoes that are about double the size of a cherry tomato, just the right size for a single-serving omelet or salad. They are also called cocktail tomatoes. (You can also grab a few cherry tomatoes from the salad bar and slice 'em, but these are better.)

- *Don't miss out on enjoying asparagus,* even though it is only sold in 1-pound (455 g) bundles; it's so wonderful and so low in carbs that it's a shame to skip it. Trim the very bottom of the stalks and "plant" your asparagus in a glass with an inch or two (2 to 5 cm) of water in it; it should stay crisp long enough for you to finish it.

- *Plan a couple of meals using a particular ingredient* within a few days of one another; for example, a mushroom omelet on Sunday and a burger smothered in sautéed mushrooms on Tuesday. Or have coleslaw at Saturday lunch and a stir-fry with cabbage for dinner on Monday.

- *Look for meats that come pre-portioned*—6- to 8-ounce (170 g to 225 g) T-bone, pork shoulder steaks, packages of just six chicken wings. You may well pay a little more than if you bought in bulk, but throwing away food that has gone bad is expensive. Depending on your freezer space, things that come frozen in portions are very helpful. I keep a bag of 8-ounce (225 g), 100 percent beef hamburger patties in my freezer. Ditto individually wrapped and frozen 6-ounce (170 g) salmon fillets and frozen shrimp.

- *Purchase cheese in single servings.* Consider Babybel, Swiss Knight, and other individual cheese bites. You can buy shredded cheddar and often crumbled blue cheese or feta from the salad bar. This avoids moldy cheese. (Two Babybel cheese snacks, shredded, are just right for one omelet.)

- *Look for single-serving guacamole in tubs* with peel-off tops. These let you have guacamole any time you like without the worry of the leftovers turning brown.

- *Find a friendly butcher.* I swear, every butcher I've ever met has been cheerful and supportive—and a big help! A Nice Meat Guy will cut you a single portion of that salmon or trout fillet, sell you just a few slices of bacon—although if you eat bacon as often as most keto dieters, you might as well buy a pound—a single pork chop or chicken breast, just one or two feta-spinach chicken sausages or 6 ounces (170 g) of ground chuck. A supermarket with a full-service meat department is a better place for grocery shopping than a Target or a Walmart.

- *Seek out packaged genuine bacon bits.* I have called for them in several recipes. You can cook bacon fresh if you prefer, but if you just want enough for a topping, packaged bacon bits are easier. Refresh them by spreading them on a plate and giving them 20 to 30 seconds in the microwave.

- *Choose rotisserie chicken* if, like me, you are not a fan of the boneless, skinless chicken breast, preferring your chicken bone-in and skin-on. No, they're not single-serving. But you can have a leg and thigh on one night, then make a chicken salad or two later in the week, or just microwave a serving to reheat. Check the seasonings: "traditional savory" and "lemon pepper" are usually fine, but barbecue is likely to have added sugar. If you're not sure, ask at the deli counter.

- *Find health food stores and big grocery stores* that sell nuts in bulk, letting you scoop out only what you need.

- *Buy tomato paste in a tube rather than a can.* Tomato paste adds a nudge of tomato flavor to foods, but it is high enough in carbs that you're unlikely to use up a whole can at a time. If you buy it in a tube, you can use just a teaspoon or two, cap it, and throw it back in the fridge.

- *Remember ice cube trays?* They are great when you use only part of a can of coconut milk or tomatoes or the like. Unless you're going to use the rest up pretty quickly, your best bet is to freeze the remainder in an ice cube tray, pop them out, and store them in a resealable bag or snap-top container. Thaw as needed.

- *Keep pork rinds from getting stale* by buying only single-serving bags of pork rinds, or get a good chip clip and use it. (Unpaid plug: I buy Clancy's pork rinds, the Aldi house brand, by the case. They're excellent quality and the price is right.) Pork rinds are not only a zero-carb snack, they are a useful ingredient in keto cooking. They are also highly nutritious. While buying them in single-serving bags can be pricey, leftover pork rinds will as soon go stale as look at you.

- *Use fresh parsley and cilantro for flavor.* Parsley keeps reasonably well in the fridge; I usually use it all up before it goes bad. Cilantro, on the other hand, is ephemeral. If you're a fan, you'll probably have to resign yourself to discarding the last third or so of each bunch. It's worth it to me. Some people mince fresh herbs in oil and freeze them in ice cube trays. If you find yourself throwing away a lot of limp herbs, this might be an interesting avenue to explore.

- *Don't make yourself crazy trying to plan* a main course and a side dish. If you're sticking to just a few grams of carb per meal, it's hard to do. Plan a side dish when you're having a plain protein—a steak, a burger, a chop, rotisserie chicken, or the like. Or don't. I've eaten just a hunk of meat many times, with no apparent harm.

- *Invest in a compact food processor.* I have a big ol' professional-grade Cuisinart, but when writing this book, I found myself using the little Black and Decker Shortcut my mom gave me for Christmas in 1986 (and which still works nicely, thank you). The small quantities of ingredients we're using often don't make contact with the S-blade of a bigger food processor.

- *Don't heat up the oven for just one serving.* I use my skillets far more than any other pans. I also use the broiler a lot; it is quick and simple.

- *Steam small amounts of vegetables* in a microwave. I have had to relearn this skill for these small quantities. It takes only 1 to 2 minutes to cook 4 to 5 stalks of asparagus or 1 cup (100 g) of cauliflower. If you're anti-microwave, you can steam, warm, or melt things on your stove, of course.

A FEW INGREDIENTS

Although most of the ingredients used in this book are familiar, a few call for a bit of explanation.

While grass-fed meat and dairy, pastured eggs, and other premium ingredients are all well and good, they are not essential to a keto diet. You can and will get the benefits of being in ketosis with grocery store meats, eggs, cheese, and butter. If you have the money to buy the superior foodstuffs, consider them a worthwhile investment. But it would be a big mistake and a darned shame to decide you cannot go keto because you can't afford to buy all super "clean" ingredients.

Regarding Sweeteners

It is entirely possible to get into a state of dietary ketosis while consuming artificial sweeteners; people have been doing it ever since Dr. Atkins published *Dr. Atkins' Diet Revolution*, commonly referred to in the community as "Atkins '72." Dr. Atkins was just fine with saccharin, then the only artificial sweetener available in the US. Come to think of it, the medical community was advocating for it before then—the ketogenic diet for seizure control was first used in the 1920s; saccharin had been around for decades by then and was used.

Because many of my readers prefer it, I mostly use stevia, monk fruit, and erythritol—natural sweeteners—in my recipes. But if you like sucralose and products containing it, it certainly can be part of a keto diet, as can other artificial sweeteners.

Sugar Alcohols
ERYTHRITOL AND MALTITOL

Erythritol is part of the sugar alcohol or polyol class of sweeteners: long-chain carbohydrates difficult for the human gut to digest or absorb. Maltitol is the polyol most commonly used in commercial sugar-free sweets, and the manufacturers like to suggest on their labels that you may discount it entirely from your net carb count. This is optimistic, at best. Roughly half of maltitol is, indeed, absorbed and must be considered part of your daily carb count.

Maltitol is also notorious for causing digestive upset, from what we will delicately call social embarrassment to severe diarrhea, depending on the dose. I know that I can get away with one to two sugar-free Reese's cups in a day, but more will make me unpleasant to be around.

These two drawbacks have caused many people to shun the sugar alcohols entirely. However, there is one sugar alcohol that is passed through the human body unchanged and has little-to-no gut effect: erythritol. This has made it a real comer on the sugar-free sweetener market.

However, erythritol comes with its own challenges. It is *endothermic*, meaning that it absorbs energy when it gets wet, creating a cooling sensation in your mouth. It is only 70 percent as sweet as sugar. Also, used in quantity, it can taste harsh.

Still, erythritol lends textural effects that can't be achieved with stevia, sucralose, or monk fruit.

ERYTHRITOL BLENDS

For quite a while, I have combined erythritol with liquid stevia, monk fruit, or sucralose. Happily, there are now blends of erythritol with stevia or monk fruit available; I like Virtue Sweetener and Natural Mate, both blends of erythritol and monk fruit. (Natural Mate also makes an erythritol-stevia blend and an erythritol-sucralose blend.) The most widely available blend is Truvia, made of erythritol and stevia. All three of these blends are roughly equivalent in sweetness, about twice as sweet as sugar. (Virtue Sweetener's label says that it is three times as sweet as sugar, but this is not my experience.) I call for these blends extensively in this book; Truvia is available in grocery stores, while Virtue and Natural Mate are, like everything these days, available online.

If you prefer, you can use straight erythritol and combine it yourself with liquid stevia, monk fruit, or sucralose. Because the blends are sweeter than straight erythritol, if you do this, you must use the same quantity of erythritol as I have called for of the blended products, then use the liquid stevia, monk fruit, or sucralose to equal that same quantity of sugar. To illustrate: I use liquid stevia that runs about 6 drops = 1 teaspoon sugar in sweetness, and about ¼ teaspoon = ¼ cup sugar in sweetness. So, if a recipe calls for ¼ cup of Natural Mate, Virtue, or Truvia, you would use ¼ cup of erythritol *plus* ¼ teaspoon of liquid stevia. Please note that this requires you to know the sweetness equivalence of your liquid sweetener!

Because, unlike the other sugar alcohols or polyols, erythritol passes through the body unchanged and completely unabsorbed, it is the one carbohydrate other than fiber that I consider legitimate to omit from net carb counts. Accordingly, the nutritional stats for this book do not account for erythritol.

LIQUID SWEETENERS

In recipes where all that is needed is a little sweetness, I use liquid sweeteners alone, because they are carb-free. Often I use flavored liquid stevias; I keep NOW and SweetLeaf brands on hand in chocolate, vanilla, English toffee, orange, and lemon. Again, these brands run 6 drops = 1 teaspoon sugar, 18 drops = 1 tablespoon sugar, ¼ teaspoon = ¼ cup sugar. If you dislike stevia, you can use an equivalent amount of liquid sucralose or monk fruit and add a few drops of flavoring extract.

Yes, you can use sucralose on a keto diet. Use the liquid instead of the granulated version, which contains maltodextrin filler. I like EZ Sweetz brand. You can also get plain liquid stevia, liquid monk fruit, and stevia/monk fruit blends, all carb-free.

It is imperative that you know the sweetness equivalence of your sweetener! If you're not sure, check the manufacturer's website, or call and ask. (EZ Sweetz liquid sucralose comes in two concentrations; check the sweetness equivalence if you purchase it.)

Chia Seeds

Chia seeds are widely touted as a "superfood." I don't know about that, but they're nutritious, with good fats, a bit of protein, and the vast majority of their carbohydrates in the form of fiber. They're also a good source of calcium, iron, thiamin, niacin, and zinc.

Because of all their fiber, chia seeds swell up when put in liquid, acting as a thickener. I've used them in a couple of pudding recipes. Those puddings have little "pearls" in them, much like tapioca pudding.

Chia seeds are available at any health food store and many grocery stores. Aldi is carrying them now! Keep 'em dry, and they'll keep for months.

Guar Gum or Xanthan Gum

These flavorless, finely milled, soluble fibers are to keto cuisine what cornstarch is to standard cooking—a thickener. However, they are far more powerful; if you try to do a one-for-one substitution for cornstarch, the results will be suitable for surfacing roads.

To use guar gum or xanthan gum, put whichever you choose in an old spice or salt shaker and keep it by the stove. When you have a sauce or soup that needs thickening, start whisking first, then sprinkle the thickener lightly over the surface. Stop when your sauce or soup is not quite as thick as you want it; it will continue to thicken on standing.

As long as these thickeners are kept dry, they will last forever. Find guar gum and xanthan gum at health food stores or online.

Coconut Milks

Because coconut milk contains highly ketogenic medium-chain triglycerides (MCTs), I use it often, both the canned stuff, which is very thick and rich, and the pourable stuff that you find in cartons along with the almond milk, soy milk, and dairy milk. When buying pourable coconut milk, read the label to make sure you're buying the unsweetened stuff. When buying canned coconut milk, buy the full-fat stuff, not the "lite" version.

If you can't have dairy products, canned coconut milk works well as a replacement for heavy cream in all kinds of recipes. You can even whip it! It won't get stiff like heavy cream, but it will get thick enough to mound, and you can spoon it over desserts or coffee.

For some reason I do not pretend to understand, canned coconut milk goes bad fairly rapidly in the fridge—you'll want to use it up within a few days—but the pourable stuff stays good considerably longer. I've used it after a couple of weeks and found it fine.

Lily's Sugar-Free Chocolate Chips

So far, Lily's brand is the only erythritol- and stevia-sweetened chocolate chips I've found. They're a health food store item and, of course, also available online. (If you can, order through your local health food store to support a local business and avoid the shipping charge.) If you prefer, you can chop up erythritol and stevia–sweetened chocolate or 85 percent cacao dark chocolate into chip-sized bits.

Coconut Oil

Because it contains medium-chain triglycerides, coconut oil is especially ketogenic. Because it is highly saturated, it keeps remarkably well, even without refrigeration.

Extra virgin coconut oil has a mild but distinct coconut odor which you may or may not enjoy in any particular dish. Just plain coconut oil is bland and can be used in the same ways as Crisco.

Coconut oil is solid at room temperature (unless it's hot and your air conditioning isn't up to snuff), so it's not useful for salad dressings, mayonnaise, and other recipes that need a liquid oil.

MCT Oil

Medium-chain triglyceride oil, commonly referred to as MCT oil, is derived from coconut oil. It is highly ketogenic and can be used directly by the muscles for fuel, creating a burst of energy. MCT oil is liquid at room temperature and bland. This makes it the perfect keto substitute for vegetable oils like safflower and soy. If you find extra virgin olive oil too strong for your taste in salad dressings, you can cut it with MCT oil. And it makes terrific mayonnaise (page 156).

Lard and Bacon Grease

It is interesting to note the correlation between vegetable oils and "shortenings" edging lard and bacon grease out of the American diet and the rise in heart disease during the twentieth century. Correlation is not causation and, of course, other changes occurred in that time, but the demonization of lard, the most traditional of fats, was and is unjust. Sadly, much of the lard available in grocery stores has been heavily processed, and some even hydrogenated. But if you can get local, small-farm lard from pasture-raised hogs, you will have fat of the highest quality, great for frying, sautéing, baking, you name it. Call around or ask around at the local farmers' market.

One problem: You may find local farmers selling lard in buckets of 4 to 5 pounds. You're unlikely to use that much up before it goes rancid. Do you have a local keto friend or two? Chip in on a bucket together and divide it up. Store in the refrigerator.

Bacon grease is just lard with a fantastic smoky, salty flavor. It improves most anything it touches. Use it for pan-broiling steaks and chops, sautéing vegetables, basting anything you're roasting, and so on. I keep my bacon grease in an old salsa jar by the stove and use it up too quickly for it to go bad.

Butter and Ghee

If you can afford grass-fed butter, go for it, but even grocery store butter is keto and nutritious. Use it for sautéing and melt it over vegetables, steaks, and eggs.

If you're lactose intolerant or otherwise avoiding dairy, consider ghee. Similar to clarified butter, ghee is butter that has had all the milk solids removed, leaving only the fats. This makes ghee less likely to spoil than butter (useful in warm climates like India) and less likely to burn. Because the milk solids have been removed, ghee is well tolerated by many people who are lactose intolerant; I know many people who avoid dairy products except for ghee.

Ghee is available in jars in stores that carry a selection of Indian foods and ingredients. Once opened, it should be refrigerated. You can make your own ghee quite easily: Melt butter over very low heat. Let the light-colored solids sink to the bottom, pour off the liquid butterfat into a container, and discard the solids.

Like butter, ghee is most nutritious if it comes from grass-fed cows.

Shirataki, Miracle Rice, and Friends

If you have tried shirataki and did not like it, please read this section: The proper preparation makes all the difference. If you have not tried shirataki, read on.

Shirataki is a traditional Japanese noodle made from the fiber glucomannan, derived from konjac or konnyaku, a root vegetable. (This is often translated as "yam," but konjac is a completely different plant.) Being made almost entirely of fiber, shirataki is very low in both carbohydrate and calories.

Shirataki comes in two basic varieties: traditional and tofu. Traditional shirataki is made entirely of glucomannan fiber. It is translucent and kind of gelatinous, really quite different from the wheat-based noodles I grew up on. I like traditional shirataki only in Asian recipes—sesame noodles, Asian soups, and the like. Tofu shirataki, as the name suggests, has a little bit of tofu added to the glucomannan. This makes it white and gives it a more tender texture than traditional shirataki. It is not identical to regular wheat-based pasta, but it's closer, and I like it in all sorts of things, from fettuccine Alfredo to tuna casserole. Both traditional and tofu shirataki come in a variety of widths and shapes.

Unlike wheat-based pasta, shirataki comes already hydrated in a pouch of liquid. To use it, snip open the pouch and dump the shirataki into a strainer in the sink. You'll notice that the liquid smells fishy. Do not panic. Rinse your noodles well and put them in a microwaveable bowl. Microwave on High for 2 minutes and drain again. Microwave for *another* 2 minutes and drain one more time. This renders the shirataki quite bland and also cooks out extra liquid that would otherwise dilute any sauce you put on it, ruining your recipe and causing you to curse.

Long noodles are considered good luck in Japan, but I find shirataki a bit too long. I snip across the noodles a few times with my kitchen shears. All of this microwaving and draining and snipping takes less time than boiling water for standard pasta.

I can get shirataki at both my local health food stores and Asian markets. If you can't find shirataki locally, you can order it online, but be aware: Shirataki does not tolerate freezing; it disintegrates into mush. This means you may not want to order it in the dead of winter. On the other hand, it keeps for months in the fridge, so if you decide you like it, go ahead and stock up.

Miracle Rice is traditional shirataki made in little bits roughly the size and shape of short-grain rice. I have also recently found shirataki couscous by Skinny Pasta—much like Miracle Rice, but the bits are a little larger. Prepare these as above; no need for the snipping part.

Wine for Cooking

A few recipes in this book call for dry white wine. I like white wine for cooking, but don't care to drink it. If you want to cook with wine you don't drink, buy the smallest box of dry white—Chardonnay, Chablis, Pinot Grigio, or the like—you can find, and stash it in the fridge to be drawn on for cooking. You can, of course, do the same with boxed dry red; we just happen to drink dry red around here.

Onions

Writing this book, I used sliced scallions and red onions from the grocery store salad bar as much as possible. But some recipes really need your standard yellow cooking onion. The problem is this: Onions are borderline vegetables, higher in carb than some, so we need to limit quantities. There is no recipe in this book that calls for a whole onion.

The only solution is to use what you need for a given recipe, put the rest in a resealable bag or snap-top container, and refrigerate it. Chances are good you'll be cooking something else that calls for onion within a few days, right?

Bonus: A cold onion won't make you cry, no matter how finely you dice it. Try it!

CHAPTER 2

EGGS, DAIRY, AND THE LIKE

All you need to know about my relationship with eggs is that I have seventeen chickens—at last count—running around my yard as I write this. What's not to love about eggs? They're highly nutritious, delicious, endlessly variable, widely available, and affordable. The busier you are, the tighter the budget, the more you should use this chapter!

I'll sneak in a suggestion here: Adding an egg or two to leftovers is a great way to turn them into a whole new meal. I've eaten fried eggs on everything from cauli-rice to meatloaf.

I consider local, small-farm, pasture-raised eggs to be worth the price. Be aware, however, that in the United States, "free-range" means only that the chickens are loose in a large barn, with some kind of access to

the outdoors, but there is no regulation as to how big the opening must be or what that outdoor area may be like, nor how long per day that access may be granted. As for eggs from chickens "fed vegetarian feed," I'm sad every time I see them. Chickens don't like that. Having kept chickens for a decade or so now, I can report that they are little dinosaurs and very much not natural vegetarians.

As for dairy, milk has 12 grams of carbohydrate per cup, so it's out. But cheese and butter are definitely in!

I'm going to assume you know how to fry, boil, and scramble eggs—and maybe even poach them. But, in my dogged determination to teach everyone who cares about good food how to make an omelet, I repeat, yet again....

DANA'S EASY OMELET METHOD

You can learn to do this quickly. Really—you can.

Before you begin, you'll need a good pan. What makes a pan good? I prefer a 7-inch (medium-size) skillet with a heavy bottom, sloping sides, and a nonstick surface. If your skillet is not-so-nonstick, give it a good shot of cooking spray before you start cooking. (If you're nervous about Teflon, check out the new ceramic nonstick pans; they're awesome.)

Here's the really important thing to know about making omelets: The word "omelet" comes from a word meaning "to laminate," or to build up layers. And that's exactly what you do; you let a layer of beaten egg cook, then you lift up the edges and tip the pan so the raw egg runs under the cooked part. You do this all around the edges, of course, so you build it up evenly. The point is, you don't just let the beaten egg lie there in the skillet and wait for it to cook through. If you do that, the bottom will be hopelessly overdone before the top is set. So, here goes:

1. First, have your filling ready. If you're using vegetables, you'll want to sauté them first. If you're using cheese, have it grated or sliced and ready to go. If you're making an omelet to use up leftovers—a great idea, by the way—warm them through in the microwave and have them standing by.

2. Coat your omelet pan well with cooking spray if it doesn't have a good nonstick surface, and set it over medium-high heat.

3. While the skillet is heating, grab your eggs (two is the perfect number for this size pan, but one or three will work, too) and a bowl. Crack the eggs into the bowl and beat them with a fork. Don't add water or milk or anything; just mix them up.

4. Test your pan to see if it's hot enough: A drop of water thrown into the pan should sizzle right away. Add a tablespoon of oil or butter, slosh it around to cover the bottom, then pour in the eggs, all at once. They should sizzle, too, and immediately start to set.

5. When the bottom layer of egg is set around the edges—and this should happen quite quickly—lift the edge using a spatula or fork and tip the pan to let the raw egg flow underneath. Do this all around the edge, until there's not enough raw egg to run.

6. Turn your burner to the lowest heat if you have a gas stove. (If you have an electric stove, you'll need a "warm" burner standing by; electric elements don't cool off fast enough for this job.) Put your filling on one-half of the omelet, cover the pan, and let it sit over very low heat for a minute or two—no more. Peek and see if the raw, shiny egg is gone from the top surface (although you can serve it that way if you like; that's how the French prefer their omelets), and the cheese, if you've used any, is melted. If not, replace the lid and let it go another minute or two.

7. When your omelet is done, slip a spatula under the half without the filling, fold it over, and then lift the whole thing onto a plate. Or you can get fancy and tip the pan, letting the filling side of the omelet slide onto the plate and folding the top over as you go, but this takes some practice.

This makes a single-serving omelet, which is just what we want for this book. If there are two of you, make two omelets rather than trying to make one big one.

Since this is a short book, I'm going to assume you can figure out cheese omelets on your own. I urge you to think of omelets whenever you have bits of leftovers to be used up, or stray stuff cluttering up the refrigerator. Some of my best omelets have been created just this way. But here are some recipes to get you started.

CREAMED CHICKEN AND SPINACH OMELET

This is probably more than you want to do on a busy morning, but it sure makes a great Sunday brunch or simple supper. You'll be grateful you don't have to share!

1. Put your omelet-making skillet over medium-low heat. Melt 1 tablespoon of the butter in the skillet and start sautéing the mushrooms and onion in it. Use your spatula to break up the mushrooms a bit more as you go.

2. When the mushrooms have darkened and exuded some liquid and the onion is translucent, add the spinach and the garlic. Sauté until the spinach is just starting to wilt, a minute or two.

3. Add the chicken, cream cheese, and heavy cream. Stir it up, and cook just until the cream cheese melts and the chicken warms through. Stir in the Parmesan, then transfer everything to a plate or bowl.

4. Give your skillet a quick wipe, put it back on the burner, and turn the heat up to medium. Let it get hot while you break your eggs into a bowl and scramble 'em up.

5. Melt the remaining 1 tablespoon of butter in the skillet and pour in the eggs. Make your omelet according to Dana's Easy Omelet Method (page 22), filling it with the chicken-mushroom-spinach mixture. Top with a little extra Parmesan if you're feeling fancy.

....

1 SERVING with: 748 Calories; 63 g Fat (75.4% calories from fat); 40 g Protein; 6 g Carbohydrate; 1 g Dietary Fiber; 5 g Net Carbs

2 tablespoons (28 g) butter, divided

3 mushrooms, sliced (about 9 slices from the salad bar)

2 tablespoons (20 g) chopped red onion (a couple of scallions, sliced, would work, too)

1 cup (30 g) loosely packed fresh spinach

½ teaspoon minced garlic

½ cup (70 g) diced cooked chicken

1 tablespoon (15 g) cream cheese

1 tablespoon (15 ml) heavy cream

2 tablespoons (5 g) grated Parmesan cheese, plus more to garnish

2 eggs

CHICKEN-SPINACH-FETA SAUSAGE OMELET

Like eggs, sausage links come individually portioned. I get the chicken-spinach-feta links at Kroger. Since they're the biggest grocery chain in the country, and they own many other chains, I figure the sausages should be pretty widely available. I buy them in packages of three and thaw the sausages one at a time.

1. Slice your sausage into rounds, add 1 tablespoon of the olive oil to your skillet, and over medium heat, start browning the sausage bits. When the sausage bits are nicely golden on both sides, transfer to a plate and reserve.

2. Put your pine nuts in the skillet and stir them over the heat for 3 to 4 minutes, until they're just touched with gold. Put them on the plate to howdy with the sausage rounds.

3. Crack your eggs into a bowl and scramble 'em. Add the remaining 1 tablespoon of olive oil to the skillet, and make your omelet according to Dana's Easy Omelet Method (page 22). Layer in the cheese first, then distribute the sausage and pine nuts evenly over that before you cover the pan.

4. When your cheese melts, it's done. Fold, plate, pour a glass of dry white wine, and kick back to have a FaceTime dinner date with your best pal.

....

1 SERVING with: 701 Calories; 59 g Fat (74.7% calories from fat); 38 g Protein; 7 g Carbohydrate; 2 g Dietary Fiber; 5 g Net Carbs

1 link uncooked chicken-spinach-feta sausage

2 tablespoons (28 ml) olive oil, divided

1 ounce (28 g) mozzarella cheese, shredded

1 tablespoon (10 g) minced onion

2 tablespoons (18 g) pine nuts

2 eggs

CHORIZO, CHEESE, AND AVOCADO OMELET

½ avocado (or substitute a single-serving tub of guacamole), peeled

2 ounces (55 g) fresh Mexican chorizo, cooked and crumbled (a few tablespoons)

1 ounce (28 g) Monterey jack cheese or Cheddar, shredded, or Mexican cheese blend

1 tablespoon (13 g) bacon grease

2 eggs

Chorizo is so good, but it doesn't generally come in single servings. I buy a link, fry it all up until done, and stash it in a snap-top container in the fridge, to draw upon over the course of a week or so.

1. Slice your avocado. We're assuming your chorizo is already cooked and crumbled and your cheese is shredded.

2. Put your egg skillet over medium heat, add the bacon grease, and melt. Crack your eggs into a bowl, and scramble them. Make your omelet according to Dana's Easy Omelet Method (page 22), layering in the cheese first, then the chorizo, with the avocado on top, before you cover the pan.

3. Fold and plate. That's it! If you'd like an appropriate libation, the new Corona Premier has just 2.6 grams of carb per bottle and is gluten-free.

....

1 SERVING with: 775 Calories; 68 g Fat (77.8% calories from fat); 34 g Protein; 10 g Carbohydrate; 3 g Dietary Fiber; 7 g Net Carbs

Note: My grocery store carries fresh Mexican chorizo in 12-ounce (340 g) packages. I find it easiest to simply cook the whole thing, use what I want right then, and refrigerate the rest for later. It is great in omelets or scrambled into eggs. Mix it with cream cheese and Mexican-blend cheese and stuff it into mushrooms. Chorizo is one of the few foods where you might not want to read the ingredients, especially if you're easily squicked out. It's generally made of what are euphemistically called "variety meats." Consider it a way to add a little nose-to-tail eating to your menu.

CLUB OMELET

Back in my low-fat, high-carb, whole-grain-eating days, a turkey club on whole wheat toast, easy on the mayo, was my favorite sandwich. Here are all the same flavors in an omelet. Instead of raw bacon, I use packaged real bacon bits, refreshed for 20 to 30 seconds in the microwave, but you can cook a couple of slices of bacon if you prefer—especially if you don't have bacon grease to cook in.

1 tablespoon (13 g) bacon grease or other fat

2 eggs

2 ounces (55 g) deli turkey (I recommend peppered turkey), sliced

1 whole Campari (cocktail) tomato or ½ small tomato, sliced, or 3–4 grape tomatoes, halved

2 tablespoons (16 g) bacon bits or 2 slices cooked bacon, crumbled

1 tablespoon (15 g) MCT mayonnaise (page 156)

1. Put your egg skillet over medium heat, add the bacon grease, and melt. Crack your eggs into a bowl and scramble them. Make your omelet according to Dana's Easy Omelet Method (page 22), cooking it in the bacon grease, of course.

2. Layer in the turkey, then the tomato. Sprinkle the bacon bits over this.

3. Fold and plate your omelet, and top with the mayonnaise.

....

1 SERVING with: 486 Calories; 40 g Fat (73.6% calories from fat); 26 g Protein; 7 g Carbohydrate; 2 g Dietary Fiber; 5 g Net Carbs

Note: That Nice Boy I Married refuses to eat any omelet that does not include cheese. If you are of his ilk, you can add a slice or two. Monterey jack, Provolone, or Swiss all go well here. If you add cheese, make it the first layer of filling, with the turkey on top, so it melts nicely.

1½ tablespoons (25 ml) balsamic vinegar

3 asparagus spears

2 eggs

1 tablespoon (14 g) butter

2 ounces (55 g) Gruyère cheese, sliced or shredded

GRUYÈRE AND ASPARAGUS OMELET WITH BALSAMIC REDUCTION

A Facebook friend told me to try making a cheese-and-asparagus omelet with a balsamic reduction. I wish I could remember who! It's simple and elegant. It's good to know that Swiss Knight individually wrapped cheese wedges are Gruyère. Two to three should serve for this omelet.

1. Put the vinegar in your smallest saucepan. Over low heat, bring to a simmer and let it cook down to half the original volume–this will take only a couple of minutes.

2. Snap the ends off the asparagus where each spear wants to break naturally. Lay the spears on a plate or in a pie plate, cover with plastic wrap or another plate, and microwave for just 1 minute on High. Uncover right away!

3. Put your egg skillet over medium heat, add the butter, and melt. Crack your eggs into a bowl and scramble them. Make your omelet according to Dana's Easy Omelet Method (page 22), layering in the Gruyère first, then the asparagus.

4. When the cheese melts, fold and plate the omelet and drizzle with the balsamic reduction.

....

1 SERVING with: 481 Calories; 39 g Fat (71.9% calories from fat); 29 g Protein; 5 g Carbohydrate; 1 g Dietary Fiber; 4 g Net Carbs

EGGS FOR A WORKING DAY BREAKFAST

2 teaspoons (9 g) butter

2 eggs

1 teaspoon water

Want eggs, even an omelet, for breakfast, but have to be at an early meeting, or get the car pool on the road? I have you covered. These fluff up nicely.

1. Coat a microwaveable bowl—a cereal bowl will do—with cooking spray. Put the butter in it and microwave on High for 20 seconds.

2. Crack the eggs into the bowl, add the water, and scramble 'em up. Now microwave (uncovered) on High for 30 to 45 seconds, stir, then microwave for another 30 to 45 seconds. Done! Eat them right out of the bowl.

....

1 SERVING with: 199 Calories; 16 g Fat (75.3% calories from fat); 11 g Protein; 1 g Carbohydrate; 0 g Dietary Fiber; 1 g Net Carbs. Analysis does not include anything you might add.

Note: *Here's the fun part: On Saturday or Sunday, stop by the salad bar at the grocery store. Scope out what looks good to go in eggs—shredded cheese, sliced scallions, sliced mushrooms, bacon bits, cubed ham, green peppers, artichoke hearts. Grab a little of this, a little of that, then throw 'em in with your eggs before microwaving them. So easy!*

HARISSA POACHED EGGS

I use Mina brand harissa paste, which I buy at Sahara Mart, my local health/international/gourmet grocery. If you can't find harissa paste locally, no doubt you can find it online. If you're a fan of spicy food, you owe it to yourself to keep a jar in the fridge. You can make this with only two eggs, if you prefer. I was hungry.

1 tablespoon (15 ml) olive oil

1½ teaspoons minced onion

¼ teaspoon minced garlic

¼ cup (60 ml) chicken broth

¼ cup (60 ml) canned tomatoes with green chiles (with juice)

2 teaspoons (10 g) harissa paste

2 kalamata olives

2 pimento-stuffed green olives

3 eggs

2 tablespoons (18 g) crumbled feta cheese

1. Coat your egg skillet with cooking spray and put it over medium heat. Add the olive oil and onion and sauté for 2 to 3 minutes, until softened.

2. Add the garlic and sauté for 30 seconds or so. Then add the broth, tomatoes, and harissa paste. Stir it all up and bring to a simmer. Let cook for a minute while you quickly slice those olives and stir them in.

3. Crack the eggs directly into the skillet, being careful not to break the yolks. Cover the skillet and let them poach until they are done to your liking—I like my whites done through but my yolks still runny, about 5 minutes.

4. Plate, sprinkle the feta on top, and dig in.

....

1 SERVING with: 423 Calories; 34 g Fat (72.6% calories from fat); 21 g Protein; 8 g Carbohydrate; 1 g Dietary Fiber; 7 g Net Carbs

Note: See those canned tomatoes with green chilies? They come in two different-sized cans, 14.5 ounces and 10 ounces. Obviously, the 10-ounce size makes more sense for the single cook; freeze the leftovers in an ice cube tray for future use.

SHAKSHUKA

A Mediterranean dish of eggs cooked in a spicy tomato sauce, shakshuka is good any time of day. I've made other versions; here I have kept the sauce to a quantity that seasons while keeping it keto. Freeze the leftover tomatoes with green chilies in an ice cube tray, and you'll have them on hand for later. In my trays, a cube is about 2 tablespoons (30 ml), or ⅛ of a cup.

1 tablespoon (15 ml) olive oil

1 tablespoon (10 g) diced onion

¼ cup (60 ml) canned tomatoes with green chiles (with juice)

1 tablespoon (15 ml) tomato sauce

½ teaspoon minced garlic

1 pinch of ground cumin

1 pinch of ground coriander

1 pinch of paprika

3 eggs

1½ teaspoons minced fresh parsley

1. Give your egg skillet a quick shot of cooking spray and put it over medium heat. Add the olive oil and onion and sauté for 2 to 3 minutes, until softened. Stir in the canned tomatoes, tomato sauce, garlic, cumin, coriander, and paprika and let it simmer for a minute.

2. Crack in the eggs, taking care not to break the yolks. Cover the skillet and let them poach until done to your liking—5 to 6 minutes gives you set whites but runny yolks.

3. Sprinkle the parsley over the whole thing, let it cook another minute, then plate.

....

1 SERVING with: 336 Calories; 27 g Fat (71.9% calories from fat); 17 g Protein; 6 g Carbohydrate; 1 g Dietary Fiber; 5 g Net Carbs

BUSY DAY SCRAMBLE

1 slice bacon

2 medium-size cremini mushrooms (or use button mushrooms, if that's what you have on hand)

1 scallion

3 eggs

1 ounce (28 g) Gruyère cheese, shredded

I made this on a day when I was too busy to get around to breakfast until 4:30—and, I might add, was darned comfortable, thanks to my ketogenic diet. Breakfast, lunch, or dinner, this is a great meal.

1. If your medium-size skillet is not nonstick, coat it with cooking spray. Put it over medium heat, add the bacon, and start frying it crisp.

2. Meanwhile, slice your mushrooms and your scallion.

3. When the bacon's done, stash it on a plate. Add the mushrooms to the grease in the pan and sauté until they start to change color, maybe 3 minutes. Add the scallion and continue sautéing until the mushrooms have softened and darkened, another 2 or 3 minutes.

4. Crack the eggs into a bowl and beat them. Pour them into the skillet, and scramble with the mushrooms and scallion until half-set. Crumble in the bacon and scramble until set to your liking.

5. Plate and top with the Gruyère. Cover with a pot lid and leave for 1 to 2 minutes to soften the cheese, then stuff it in your face.

....

1 SERVING with: 364 Calories; 26 g Fat (64.1% calories from fat); 28 g Protein; 4 g Carbohydrate; 1 g Dietary Fiber; 3 g Net Carbs

GUACAMOLE TOAST WITH EGG

You might think that this would be only one serving, but That Nice Boy I Married and I each were quite full with one toast round, one serving of guac, and one fried egg. If it's just you, tuck your second toast round in a baggie and refrigerate it for tomorrow morning. Bacon tastes great with this, if you've got room left.

You'll want to buy the little single-serving guacamole tubs with the peel-off lids. So great to have guac on hand all the time!

1. Make your toast first. While it's frying, heat your egg skillet over medium heat and fry your eggs.

2. Spread each toast round with 1 ounce of guacamole, top with an egg, and breakfast is served. Or lunch. Or dinner. Who cares?

....

2 SERVINGS, each with: 336 Calories; 28 g Fat (73.8% calories from fat); 16 g Protein; 7 g Carbohydrate; 1 g Dietary Fiber; 6 g Net Carb

Hot, Buttery Toast Made from Mix (page 127)

2 eggs

1 tablespoon (14 g) butter (in addition to the butter you use for the toast)

2 ounces (55 g) guacamole (or 2 single-serving tubs)

HOT CHIA CEREAL

1½ tablespoons (16.5 g) chia seeds

¼ cup (60 ml) water

½ cup (120 ml) canned coconut milk

2 egg yolks (feed the whites to the dog)

⅜ teaspoon English toffee–flavored stevia

Tiny pinch of salt

I was going for something between a custard and a pudding. But when I tasted it, debating how to make it thicker, I realized that this was like the yummiest hot cereal ever. Perfect comfort food, especially on a snowy day.

1. Put the chia seeds in a good-sized microwaveable bowl; I used a small glass mixing bowl. Add the water and let them soak for at least 10 minutes, and overnight isn't crazy—and it saves time in the morning.

2. Whisk in the coconut milk, egg yolks, stevia, and salt. Microwave on 70 percent power for 1 minute at a time, whisking well in between each heating. When it's hot through and thickened up to a porridge consistency—it takes about 5 minutes in my microwave—it's ready.

....

1 SERVING with: 448 Calories; 41 g Fat (79.0% calories from fat); 11 g Protein; 13 g Carbohydrate; 8 g Dietary Fiber; 5 g Net Carbs

CHAPTER 3

SOUPS AND SIDES

The easiest keto side dishes are salad from the salad bar or simple steamed vegetables with butter and perhaps a squeeze of lemon juice. I am a fan of both.

But we run into the "If you have this, you don't have carb room left for that" principle. Soup as a starter or vegetables as a side dish only make sense if you're having a carb-free main dish, such as grilled steak or roasted chicken.

On the other hand, a simple meal of soup can be heart- and tummy-warming. With the teeny appetite that often results from ketosis, it may well be all you want. And I've been known to make a light meal of a tasty vegetable dish, like green beans amandine, or one of my rice-a-phony dishes (pages 56 to 57), or UnPotato Salad (page 51), which makes them not really sides, but geez, I have to call them something.

So, whether you eat them with a slab of meat or on their own, here are some soups, hot vegetable dishes, and side salads.

ABOUT BROTH OR STOCK

Bone broth is currently a "hot" food, and rightly so. It's very nutritious stuff. It's also pricey if you buy it, rather than make it. Fortunately, it's dead simple to make. I save all my chicken bones, no matter how naked they've been picked, in a plastic grocery sack in the freezer. When I have enough to fill my slow cooker, I dump them in, cover them with water, add about a teaspoon of salt and a couple of tablespoons of vinegar—cider or wine—slap on the lid, and set it to low. I then let it sit for—no kidding—a couple of days. Let it cool, strain, then freeze in containers to draw on as needed. If you lack chicken bones, you can use backs and necks with great results.

However, this requires sufficient freezer space to store your bone broth, and many single people lack it. I won't pay full price for packaged bone broth. Buy good packaged broth or stock; I like Kitchen Basics or Costco's Kirkland brand. To make it more like homemade bone broth, pour a whole quart into a saucepan and sprinkle 2 teaspoons (5 g) of unflavored gelatin on top. Let it sit for 5 minutes for the gelatin to soften, then bring to a simmer and let it cook until it's reduced by about 25 percent. Stash it in the fridge if you'll use it up quickly, or freeze in single servings if you won't.

If even that's too much trouble, skip the reduction step and add a little bouillon concentrate—I like Better Than Bouillon paste—to your boxed stock. This will bolster the frail flavor of packaged stocks.

CREAM OF CHICKEN SOUP WITH POACHED EGGS

This light, simple dish will warm your heart along with your tummy. Variable, too! Feel free to add a little curry powder, a teaspoon of Italian seasoning, a smidge of garlic, a splash of white wine, some snipped tarragon, or whatever floats your boat.

1½ cups (355 ml) chicken broth

½ teaspoon chicken bouillon concentrate (optional)

2 very fresh eggs

Salt and pepper

¼ cup (60 ml) heavy cream

2 tablespoons (10 g) grated Parmesan cheese

1. Pour your broth into a medium-size saucepan and put it over medium-low heat. Add the chicken bouillon concentrate, if using—I think it improves the flavor, but some people object to it—and bring just to a simmer.

2. In the meanwhile, crack your eggs into a custard cup—this way if a yolk breaks, you can save it for another recipe. When the broth is simmering, turn it down so it's just below a simmer, add salt and pepper to taste, and slip in the eggs. Poach until set to your liking—I give mine 7 minutes.

3. While the eggs are poaching, put the cream in a bowl. When the eggs are done, transfer them to the bowl with a slotted spoon. Pour in the broth, top with the Parmesan, and supper is ready.

....

1 SERVING with: 442 Calories; 36 g Fat (74.0% calories from fat); 24 g Protein; 5 g Carbohydrate; 0 g Dietary Fiber; 5 g Net Carbs

1½ cups (355 ml) chicken broth

¼ cup (60 ml) salsa (Read the labels! Too many have added sugar)

⅔ teaspoon chili powder

⅓ teaspoon ground cumin

⅓ teaspoon paprika

⅓ teaspoon dried oregano

Salt and pepper

¼ cup (35 g) diced cooked chicken

1 ounce (28 g) guacamole (1 single-serving tub)

2 tablespoons (14 g) shredded Monterey jack cheese or Mexican cheese blend

Chopped fresh cilantro (optional)

SOPA MEXICANA, RÁPIDO Y FÁCIL

Or Quick and Easy Mexican Soup. Or Mexican-ish, at any rate. You can use boneless, skinless chicken breast for this, but you'll have quite a lot of unused breast left over. I go with chicken from the salad bar or leftover rotisserie chicken.

1. Combine the broth, salsa, chili powder, cumin, paprika, and oregano in a saucepan over medium heat. Bring to a simmer, add salt and pepper to taste, and stir in the chicken. Adjust the heat so it stays just at a simmer for 5 minutes or so.

2. Pour your soup into a bowl. Scoop your guac into the center, scatter the cheese over it, and sprinkle the cilantro, if using. Done!

....

1 SERVING with: 306 Calories; 20 g Fat (57.6% calories from fat); 23 g Protein; 10 g Carbohydrate; 3 g Dietary Fiber; 7 g Net Carbs

CURRIED CREAM OF CHICKEN SOUP

I've published versions of this before. It's so simple, so good, and so perfect for this book that I couldn't skip it. I usually eat this as-is, but feel free to add diced cooked chicken, if you want something heartier. Grab the chicken from the salad bar, of course.

1. In a medium-size saucepan over medium-low heat, melt ½ tablespoon of the butter. Add the almonds and stir until they're a pretty gold. Transfer to a small plate and reserve.

2. Put the remaining ½ tablespoon of butter in the pan and add the curry powder. Sauté for just 1 to 2 minutes, until fragrant. Add the chicken broth and coconut milk. Turn the heat up to medium-high, bring to a boil, then turn down to a simmer.

3. Stir in the bouillon concentrate, if using, and salt and pepper to taste. Serve with the toasted almonds on top.

....

1 SERVING with: 428 Calories; 42 g Fat (84.6% calories from fat); 10 g Protein; 8 g Carbohydrate; 2 g Dietary Fiber; 6 g Net Carbs

1 tablespoons (14 g) butter, divided

1 tablespoon (7 g) sliced almonds

1½ teaspoons curry powder

1 cup (235 ml) chicken broth

½ cup (120 ml) canned coconut milk

½ teaspoon chicken bouillon concentrate (optional)

Salt and pepper

CALIFORNIA SOUP FOR ONE

1 cup (235 ml) chicken broth

2 ounces (55 g) guacamole (2 single-serving tubs)

Salt and pepper

In *500 Low-Carb Recipes*, I included a recipe for California Soup—simply hot chicken broth and ripe avocado blended together. This is similar, but leaves you with no leftover avocado to use up.

Put the broth and guac in a blender and process until smooth; pour into a saucepan. (Or use a stick blender right in the saucepan.) Put over medium heat, heat through, add salt and pepper to taste, and pour into a mug. Done.

....

1 SERVING with: 127 Calories; 10 g Fat (66.5% calories from fat); 6 g Protein; 5 g Carbohydrate; 1 g Dietary Fiber; 4 g Net Carbs

SOPA DE POLLO Y QUESO

Super-simple—you can make it in the bowl or a big mug, if you like. If you want it heartier, add some diced cooked chicken, whether from the salad bar or leftover rotisserie chicken.

1 cup (235 ml) chicken broth

½ cup (120 ml) queso dip or sauce (read the labels to find the one with the fewest carbs and least additives)

Salt and pepper

Guar gum or xanthan gum (optional)

Hot sauce (optional)

Minced fresh cilantro (optional)

1. Heat the broth and queso together, stirring until smooth. Add salt and pepper to taste. Thicken a tad with your guar or xanthan shaker, if you like.

2. Add a splash of hot sauce and/or a sprinkle of cilantro if you like, but it's soothing and good as-is.

....

1 SERVING with: 292 Calories; 22 g Fat (65.3% calories from fat); 22 g Protein; 5 g Carbohydrate; 0 g Dietary Fiber; 5 g Net Carbs

COLESLAW FOR ONE

This will turn any simple meat dish—a rotisserie chicken, a pan-broiled pork steak, or the like—into a meal. Why not deli coleslaw? Because it's loaded with sugar, that's why. With the MCT Mayo in it, this will generate plenty of ketones.

1 tablespoon (15 g) sour cream

1 tablespoon (15 g) MCT Mayo (page 156)

1 teaspoon cider vinegar

½ teaspoon brown mustard

1 pinch of salt

Liquid stevia, monk fruit, or sucralose to equal ½ to 1 teaspoon sugar

1 cup (85 g) coleslaw mix

1. Mix together the sour cream, mayo, vinegar, mustard, salt, and sweetener. This, unsurprisingly, is your dressing.

2. Put your coleslaw mix in a medium-size mixing bowl, pour on the dressing, and stir it up. Done!

....

1 SERVING with: 133 Calories; 15 g Fat (94.5% calories from fat); 1 g Protein; 1 g Carbohydrate; Trace Dietary Fiber; 1 g Net Carbs

SALAD BAR UNPOTATO SALAD

UnPotato Salad—made with cauliflower—is a favorite of mine. But hitherto I have made it in quantity, for gatherings. How do you make just a couple of servings? My grocery store's salad bar had everything needed but the celery and the mayo. This is two servings as a side dish, but I've been known to eat the whole thing as a meal.

    I have often used red onion, rather than scallions, in this salad. My salad bar offers both, but the red onion is always in slices that need further dicing, while the scallions are sliced perfectly for the purpose. Take your pick!

1 cup (100 g) cauliflower florets

½ cup (68 g) chopped hard-cooked egg

¼ cup (40 g) chopped scallion or diced red onion

1 celery rib (or about ⅓ cup [40 g] diced celery, if your salad bar offers it)

3 tablespoons (45 g) MCT Mayo (page 156)

Liquid stevia, sucralose, or monk fruit to equal just a pinch of sugar (probably 1 drop) (optional)

1. Head to the nearest salad bar; you'll be eyeballing the quantities. Do yourself a favor and grab the smallest cauliflower bits you can find from the salad bar. Put them in one container. Put the chopped egg and scallion in another. Take them home and stick 'em in the fridge, ready to make UnPotato Salad at will.

2. Okay, it's time. Cut up any cauliflower bits as needed to ½ inch (1 cm) or smaller. Put them in a microwaveable mixing bowl, add a teaspoon or two of water, cover with a plate, and microwave on High for just 2 minutes. (The timing will depend a bit on your microwave and the size of your bowl, but 3 minutes is too long in my microwave.) Uncover as soon as the microwave beeps, drain, and stick it in the fridge for 5 minutes to cool.

3. While the cauliflower is cooling, dice your celery rib.

4. When the cauliflower cools down to lukewarm, add the celery, hard-cooked egg, scallion, mayo, and sweetener, if using. Stir it up. Done!

....

2 SERVINGS, each with: 220 Calories; 21 g Fat (82.2% calories from fat); 6 g Protein; 5 g Carbohydrate; 2 g Dietary Fiber; 3 g Net Carbs

ZOODLES FOR ONE

1 small zucchini

Salt

1 tablespoon (15 ml) olive oil

½ teaspoon minced garlic (optional)

½ teaspoon dried oregano (optional)

Zoodles—zucchini noodles—are hugely popular among the keto set. I prefer tofu shirataki for most purposes, but feel free to substitute these for shirataki noodles in any recipe in this book.

1. Simply run your zukes through your spiral cutter, piling your zoodles in a mixing bowl. Salt the zoodles, tossing as you go. Let them sit for 15 to 20 minutes, until they begin to release liquid.

2. Use clean hands to squeeze your zoodles to get out the excess liquid and drain them well.

3. Put your big, heavy skillet over medium-high heat and add the olive oil. When it's hot, add the zoodles, and toss them in the olive oil just until good and hot clear through. Stir in the garlic and oregano, if using, and cook for just another minute. Don't let them get mushy!

....

1 SERVING with: 151 Calories; 14 g Fat (77.4% calories from fat); 2 g Protein; 7 g Carbohydrate; 3 g Dietary Fiber; 4 g Net Carbs

CAULI-RICE FROM FROZEN RICED CAULIFLOWER

For years and years I have been running raw cauliflower through the shredding blade of my food processor to make cauli-rice, but that seems like a lot of work for just one serving. You can get riced cauliflower in the produce department of most grocery stores these days, but unless you eat it daily, you're likely to wind up tossing half the bag. Go with the frozen stuff! Here's how to cook just 1 cup of frozen cauli-rice, whether to use as a bed for a dish with a good sauce, or in place of Miracle Rice in one of my recipes.

Put your riced cauliflower, still frozen, in a cereal bowl and put a small plate or saucer on top. Microwave on High for 1 minute. Uncover, stir, and give it another 30 to 60 seconds. Don't overcook! Cauli-rice is all about the texture.

....

1 SERVING with: 56 Calories; 0 g Fat (0.0% calories from fat); 3 g Protein; 8 g Carbohydrate; 6 g Dietary Fiber; 2 g Net Carbs

Note: If you want to make your own Fauxtatoes instead of buying frozen pureed cauliflower, riced cauliflower is a fine place to start. Microwave it for 5 minutes, drain it really well, then run it through your food processor or mash it with a stick blender, adding a little cream cheese and butter in the process.

1 cup (85 g) frozen riced cauliflower

PARMESAN BEANS

I confess to having made this with frozen cross-cut green beans, thawed. Feel free to use fresh if you prefer. Just cut them into 2- to 3-inch (5 cm to 7 cm) lengths.

1. Put a skillet over medium-high heat. When it's good and hot, add the olive oil and green beans and sauté for 2 to 3 minutes, just until you see a few brown spots forming.

2. Turn the heat to medium-low. Stir in the water and garlic and immediately cover the pan. Let the beans steam until just tender, 6 to 7 minutes.

3. Stir in the Parmesan, add salt and pepper to taste, and they're done.

....

2 SERVINGS, each with: 161 Calories; 15 g Fat (81.4% calories from fat); 3 g Protein; 5 g Carbohydrate; 2 g Dietary Fiber; 3 g Net Carbs

2 tablespoons (28 ml) olive oil

1 cup (100 g) cut green beans

3 tablespoons (45 ml) water

½ teaspoon minced garlic

2 tablespoons (10 g) grated Parmesan cheese

Salt and pepper

CHICKEN AND ALMOND RICE-A-PHONY FOR ONE

½ teaspoon chicken bouillon concentrate

1 tablespoon (15 ml) water

1 tablespoon (14 g) butter

1 tablespoon (7 g) sliced almonds

1 cup (85 g) frozen riced cauliflower

1 tablespoon (10 g) chopped scallion (1 scallion)

2 teaspoons (2 g) minced fresh parsley

Frozen riced cauliflower is such a boon to the small-batch cook! I don't know why you'd bother to shred your own. All my local grocery stores carry it, even Aldi. You can turn this into a light meal by stirring in diced leftover chicken or topping it with a couple of fried eggs. Yum.

1. Dissolve the chicken bouillon concentrate in the water. Put by the stove.

2. Put a medium-size skillet over medium-low heat, add the butter, and melt. Add the almonds and stir until they're golden, 4 to 5 minutes. Transfer the almonds to a plate, leaving as much butter in the pan as you can.

3. Throw in the riced cauliflower, still frozen. Stir in the chicken bouillon mixture and cover the skillet. Let it cook for 2 to 3 minutes, until thawed.

4. Stir in the scallion and parsley, replace the cover, and let it cook for another 90 seconds or so.

5. Return the almonds to the skillet, stir it up one more time, and you're done.

....

1 SERVING with: 216 Calories; 16 g Fat (69.9% calories from fat); 5 g Protein; 11 g Carbohydrate; 6 g Dietary Fiber; 5 g Net Carbs

BEEF AND WALNUT RICE-A-PHONY FOR ONE

Tired of tossed green salad next to your steak? Give this a try. Or if you have leftover steak, slice it up and stir it in!

1. In a medium-size skillet over medium heat, fry the bacon crisp. Remove from the skillet and reserve on a plate, leaving the grease in the skillet. Add the 1 tablespoon additional bacon grease to the skillet.

2. Fry the walnuts in the bacon grease for 4 to 5 minutes, just until they smell toasty. Scoop them out and add 'em to the plate with the bacon.

3. Now throw the onion and mushroom in the skillet and fry 'em for just a couple of minutes. While that's happening, mix the beef bouillon concentrate with the water.

4. Throw the riced cauliflower, still frozen, in with the onion and mushrooms. Stir in the bouillon mixture and cover the skillet. Let it cook for 3 to 4 minutes, until thawed. Use this time to mince the parsley and sun-dried tomato, if you need to.

5. Add the parsley and sun-dried tomato to the skillet along with the oil from the tomatoes. Stir in the walnuts, plate, and crumble the bacon over the top.

....

1 SERVING with: 277 Calories; 21 g Fat (69.3% calories from fat); 8 g Protein; 13 g Carbohydrate; 7 g Dietary Fiber; 6 g Net Carbs

1 slice bacon

1 tablespoon (13 g) bacon grease

1 tablespoon (8 g) chopped walnuts

1 tablespoon (10 g) minced onion

1 mushroom or a handful of mushroom slices from the salad bar, chopped

½ teaspoon beef bouillon concentrate

1 tablespoon (15 ml) water

1 cup (85 g) frozen riced cauliflower

2 teaspoons (2 g) minced fresh parsley

1 oil-packed sun-dried tomato half, minced, plus a teaspoon of the oil

CHAPTER 4

MAIN DISH SALADS

Do you love main dish salads? They have long been the dieter's mainstay. It is disconcerting, therefore, to realize that we have to keep an eye even on nonstarchy vegetables if we're keeping our carbs to ketogenic levels. Which is just what I have done here.

This, by the way, is the reason that main dish salads are not always the best choice for us on restaurant menus. Restaurant chain nutrition charts can be revealing and dismaying. You know to skip the croutons or tortilla strips, but even then you may find your favorites have more carbs than you want to "spend" that way.

You have your own favorite tuna salad and egg salad recipes, right? Make them with MCT Mayo and watch your ketone levels soar!

Following are some other salad ideas.

Note: The US has had several recalls of romaine lettuce due to E. coli *risks. A simple online search will let you know if there's currently a recall in your region.*

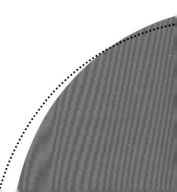

SALMON-SPINACH CAESAR SALAD

Some alliteration, huh? And this is quite a salad. That Nice Boy I Married, generally not a fan of the main dish salad, gave this top marks. My grocery store sells trimmings of lox that they've smoked in-store far cheaper than the packaged stuff, and better, too. That's what I've used here. Buy the spinach from the salad bar; they may have shredded Parmesan, too.

2 teaspoons (9 g) butter

2 tablespoons (16 g) chopped walnuts

2 cups (60 g) loosely packed baby spinach

¼ cup (60 ml) Caesar Salad Dressing (page 158)

6 ounces (170 g) lox, chopped into bite-size pieces

2 tablespoons (10 g) shredded Parmesan cheese

1 scallion, thinly sliced, or a little scallion from the salad bar

1 teaspoon capers

1. In a small skillet over medium-low heat, melt the butter. Add the walnuts and stir them in the butter until they smell toasty, about 5 minutes. Set aside.

2. Put your spinach in a salad or mixing bowl and add the dressing. Toss to coat. Pile the spinach on a plate.

3. Top with the lox and Parmesan cheese, then artfully sprinkle the scallion, capers, and those toasted walnuts over the top before inhaling.

....

1 SERVING with: 702 Calories; 55 g Fat (71.2% calories from fat); 41 g Protein; 9 g Carbohydrate; 3 g Dietary Fiber; 6 g Net Carbs

CHICKEN, ASPARAGUS, AND BACON SALAD

1 (8-ounce [225 g]) package Miracle Rice or shirataki couscous

6 asparagus spears

¼ cup (32 g) bacon bits

1½ teaspoons butter

2 tablespoons (14 g) sliced or slivered almonds

1 cup (140 g) diced cooked chicken

¼ cup (60 ml) olive oil

3 tablespoons (45 ml) lemon juice

¼ teaspoon minced garlic

Salt and pepper

Note: Skinny Pasta makes a good shirataki couscous that's worth seeking out.

This makes two servings because I didn't want to leave you with half a packet of unused Miracle Rice or shirataki couscous. Take the second serving to work for lunch tomorrow! Feel free to make this with cauli-rice (page 53) if you prefer.

1. Prepare the Miracle Rice or shirataki couscous according to the instructions on page 17.

2. Snap the ends off the asparagus spears where they break naturally. Lay them on your cutting board and slice them on the diagonal into 1-inch (2.5 cm) bits. Put them in a microwaveable bowl with a teaspoon of water. Put a small plate or saucer on top.

3. When the Miracle Rice has been microwaved and drained for the last time, let it sit uncovered to cool for a few minutes. Meanwhile, give your asparagus 1 minute in the microwave on High and uncover immediately.

4. See that little plate you just removed from the asparagus? Spread your bacon bits on it, and microwave them for 20 to 30 seconds to refresh.

5. Put a small skillet over medium-low heat, add the butter, and melt. Add the almonds and sauté, stirring frequently, until golden, about 5 minutes.

6. Okay, assembly time! Put your Miracle Rice in a mixing bowl. Snip up your chicken with a kitchen shears and add to the bowl, along with the asparagus. Add the olive oil, lemon juice, and garlic to the mixing bowl, and stir until it's all evenly coated. Add salt and pepper to taste.

7. If you have a companion, stir in the bacon bits and almonds now. If you're saving half for later, dish up today's portion and top with half the bacon and half the almonds. Put the remaining salad in a snap-top container, and the bacon and almonds into another, or put them in a resealable bag and add at serving time.

....

2 SERVINGS, each with: 631 Calories; 55 g Fat (75.9% calories from fat); 29 g Protein; 10 g Carbohydrate; 3 g Dietary Fiber; 7 g Net Carbs

CHICKEN-FETA SAUSAGE WITH CUCUMBER SALAD

My Kroger always has these sausages available, and they're the biggest grocery chain in the country, so I figure most of you will be able to find them. They're super-tasty and quick and easy to make. I've taken to buying what are labeled as "baby" cucumbers. They are just the right size for making one or two servings.

¾ cup (78 g) thinly sliced cucumber

1 tablespoon (10 g) minced red onion

2 tablespoons (28 ml) olive oil, divided

2 teaspoons (10 ml) red wine vinegar

¼ teaspoon minced garlic

1 uncooked chicken-spinach-feta sausage

1 pepperoncini pepper

5 kalamata olives, pitted

Salt and pepper

1. Put the cucumber, onion, 1 tablespoon of the olive oil, the vinegar, and garlic in a bowl and stir it all up.

2. Give your small skillet a squirt of cooking spray and put it over medium heat. Add the remaining 1 tablespoon of olive oil, and start cooking your sausage.

3. Meanwhile, pull the stem and seeds out of your pepperoncini and thinly slice it crosswise. Slice your olives, too. Don't forget to turn your sausage!

4. When the sausage is golden, after 6 to 8 minutes, transfer it to your cutting board and let it cool just a little while you stir up your cucumber salad, add salt and pepper to taste, then pile it on a salad plate.

5. Slice your sausage into ¼-inch (6.5 mm) rounds and top the salad with them. Scatter the pepperoncini and olives over the top.

....

1 SERVING with: 449 Calories; 40 g Fat (77.6% calories from fat); 18 g Protein; 8 g Carbohydrate; 2 g Dietary Fiber; 6 g Net Carbs

GINGER-LIME CHICKEN SALAD

2 teaspoons (10 ml) olive oil or MCT oil (see page 16)

1 tablespoon (9 grams) shelled pumpkin seeds (pepitas)

2 tablespoons (30 g) MCT Mayo (page 156)

2 teaspoons (3 g) diced red onion

½ teaspoon grated and peeled fresh ginger root

½ teaspoon minced garlic

½ teaspoon soy sauce

1 teaspoon lime juice

1 dash of sriracha (optional)

¾ cup (105 g) diced cooked chicken

¼ cup (30 g) diced celery

Salt and pepper

Not your standard chicken salad! This is good wrapped in lettuce leaves, or you can be really revolutionary and eat it with a fork.

1. Put a small skillet over medium-low heat. Add the oil and the pumpkin seeds, and stir until they turn golden and swell a bit in the middle, 4 to 5 minutes. Remove from the heat, sprinkle lightly with salt, and reserve.

2. To make the dressing, combine the mayo, onion, ginger root, garlic, soy sauce, lime juice, and sriracha in your food processor or blender and process until the onion is pulverized.

3. Put the chicken and celery in a mixing bowl, add the dressing, and stir to coat. Dish it up and top with the pumpkin seeds.

....

1 SERVING with: 728 Calories; 64 g Fat (77.7% calories from fat); 37 g Protein; 4 g Carbohydrate; 1 g Dietary Fiber; 3 g Net Carbs

CHICKEN, ARTICHOKE, AND COUSCOUS SALAD

The moment I spotted a jar of artichoke bruschetta at the grocery store, this dish sprang, fully formed, into my mind. Sure, the artichoke bruschetta is meant to be spread on toasted baguette. Why should we be limited by the expectations of others?

Skinny Pasta makes the shirataki couscous; it's like Miracle Rice, but in bits about twice as big. Or use cauli-rice, if you prefer.

1. Prepare the Miracle Rice according to the instructions on page 17.

2. While that's happening, put your pine nuts in a small skillet over medium-low heat and stir until golden, 4 to 5 minutes. Remove from the heat.

3. Let your Miracle Rice cool a bit—or not; you can eat this as a hot dish rather than a salad, if you like.

4. Add the chicken, artichoke spread, lemon juice, and Parmesan to the Miracle Rice, and stir it all up. Add salt and pepper to taste.

5. Pile it on a plate, top with the parsley and toasted pine nuts, and dig in.

....

1 SERVING with: 530 Calories; 43 g Fat (71.7% calories from fat); 29 g Protein; 8 g Carbohydrate; 4 g Dietary Fiber; 4 g Net Carbs

1 (8-ounce [225 g]) package Miracle Rice or shirataki couscous

2 tablespoons (18 g) pine nuts

½ cup (70 g) diced cooked chicken

¼ cup (60 g) artichoke bruschetta spread

1 tablespoon (15 ml) lemon juice

2 tablespoons (10 g) grated Parmesan cheese

Salt and pepper

1 tablespoon (4 g) minced fresh parsley

LATE SUMMER SALAD

½ cup (52 g) thinly sliced cucumber, or 1 baby cucumber, sliced

½ cup (70 g) diced cooked chicken

¼ cup (45 g) diced tomato, or 1 Campari (cocktail) tomato, diced

1 tablespoon (10 g) minced red onion

1 tablespoon (4 g) minced fresh parsley

3 tablespoons (27 g) crumbled feta cheese

3 green olives, pitted and sliced

3 kalamata olives, pitted and sliced

1 tablespoon (15 ml) extra virgin olive oil

1½ teaspoons red wine vinegar

¼ teaspoon minced garlic

Salt and pepper

If you can get your cucumber, chicken, tomato, and onion from the salad bar, so much the better! This was inspired by the marinated feta-and-olives I got at the antipasto bar at my local grocery store—highly recommended if you can find it. If your grocery store doesn't carry something of the kind, just use crumbled feta from a tub or the salad bar and olives from a jar.

Also good for this are baby cucumbers and Campari tomatoes, which are about double to triple the size of cherry tomatoes, perfect for one serving. If you use these, you may as well just cut up one of each, rather than measuring.

Super-simple! Just throw the cucumber, chicken, tomato, onion, parsley, feta, and olives in a mixing bowl. Add the oil, vinegar, and garlic. Season to taste with salt and pepper and it's ready!

....

1 SERVING with: 507 Calories; 41 g Fat (72.9% calories from fat); 26 g Protein; 8 g Carbohydrate; 2 g Dietary Fiber; 6 g Net Carbs

STEAK AND BLUE CHEESE SALAD

Stuck with leftover steak? Awww, poor you! Stop by the salad bar and grab the veggies—and even the blue cheese, if your salad bar is up-and-coming. You can be in front of the tube and eating a killer meal in 5 minutes flat.

1. Warm the steak if you like, though I wouldn't bother. Thinly slice across the grain.

2. Put the romaine in a mixing bowl or salad bowl, pour on the dressing, and toss until it's all well-coated. Pile it on a plate.

3. Scatter the tomatoes and red onion over the lettuce. Lay the steak slices over that, and top with the blue cheese. Pour a glass of cabernet and grab the remote!

....

1 SERVING with: 512 Calories; 43 g Fat (75.2% calories from fat); 24 g Protein; 8 g Carbohydrate; 3 g Dietary Fiber; 5 g Net Carbs

4 ounces (115 g) leftover steak, sliced

2 cups (94 g) chopped romaine lettuce

2 tablespoons (30 ml) balsamic vinaigrette

1 Campari (cocktail) or small tomato, cut into wedges, or 3–4 cherry or grape tomatoes, halved

1 tablespoon (10 g) minced red onion

3 tablespoons (23 g) crumbled blue cheese

WASABI CRAB SALAD LETTUCE WRAPS

½ cup (59 g) cooked lump crabmeat, fresh or good-quality canned

2 tablespoons (30 g) MCT Mayo (page 156)

1 teaspoon wasabi paste

1 baby carrot, shredded, or 2 tablespoons (10 g) shredded carrot from the salad bar

½ avocado

Salt

12 butter lettuce leaves

Doesn't have to be lettuce, though. You could just pile it on the avocado slices and eat it with a fork. Or you could pile it on a bed of lettuce from the salad bar.

1. Simply mix the crabmeat with the mayo, wasabi, and carrot.

2. Peel and slice the avocado into six slices.

3. Lay an avocado slice on a couple of lettuce leaves, spread some crab salad on it, wrap, and eat. Repeat!

....

1 SERVING with: 435 Calories; 40 g Fat (77.3% calories from fat); 16 g Protein; 11 g Carbohydrate; 4 g Dietary Fiber; 7 g Net Carbs

SOUTHWESTERN TUNA ON AVOCADO WITH CHIPOTLE CREMA

I was looking for something new to do with canned tuna, and this turned out to be delicious. But if you want a hot entrée, you can sprinkle the seasonings on a tuna steak, pan-broil or grill it, and serve it on the avocado slices with the crema on top.

Chipotle Crema (page 165)

5 ounces (140 g) canned tuna in olive oil

¼ teaspoon chili powder

⅛ teaspoon ground cumin

⅛ teaspoon dried oregano

Salt

½ avocado, peeled

2 teaspoons (1.2 g) minced fresh cilantro (optional)

1. Make your Chipotle Crema first.

2. Lightly drain the tuna—you want some of the oil, but you don't want the finished dish to be unappetizingly oily. Sprinkle in the chili powder, cumin, and oregano; add a tablespoon of the Chipotle Crema; and stir until evenly seasoned. Salt to taste.

3. Slice the avocado and fan the slices on a plate. Pile the tuna on top, and spoon the rest of the Chipotle Crema over it. Top with the cilantro, if using. Done!

....

1 SERVING with: 546 Calories; 37 g Fat (59.1% calories from fat); 45 g Protein; 11 g Carbohydrate; 3 g Dietary Fiber; 8 g Net Carbs

TOMATO AND AVOCADO EGG SALAD

1 tablespoon (15 g) MCT Mayo (page 156)

1 tablespoon (15 g) sour cream

1½ teaspoons lemon juice

2 dashes hot sauce, such as Frank's, Tabasco, or Louisiana, or more to taste

Salt

1½ cups (45 g) loosely packed baby spinach

1 tablespoon (10 g) diced red onion

1 tablespoon (4 g) minced fresh parsley

1 Campari (cocktail) tomato, 3–4 cherry or grape tomatoes, or ½ small tomato, diced

½ avocado, peeled and diced

2 hard-cooked eggs, peeled and sliced

Such a pretty salad with all bright colors! And you can get most of it from the salad bar. Heck, if you don't care whether your eggs are in neat yellow-and-white circles, you can use chopped egg from the salad bar, too.

1. First make your dressing: Whisk together the mayo, sour cream, lemon juice, hot sauce, and salt to taste.

2. Put your spinach in a mixing or salad bowl, along with the onion and parsley. Pour on the dressing and toss until everything is evenly coated.

3. Pile the salad on a plate. Top prettily with the tomato, avocado, and egg slices.

....

1 SERVING with: 476 Calories; 41 g Fat (73.9% calories from fat); 17 g Protein; 15 g Carbohydrate; 5 g Dietary Fiber; 10 g Net Carbs

CHAPTER 5

HOT ENTRÉES

This is by far the biggest chapter in the book. Why?

Theoretically, hot entrées are the easiest part of a keto diet. All you have to do is eat plain meat, poultry, or fish and you'll be in zero-carb territory. Indeed, if you don't crave variety, there is no reason not to eat meat—especially fatty meat—and pretty darned close to nothing else. I know a few straight carnivores who seem to be doing just fine, thank you very much. You might throw in a little liver now and then for extra vitamins.

If you're looking for convenience foods, consider rotisserie chicken. You can have one or two meals of chicken and a salad, then use the leftovers in main dish salads, soups, and other dishes. Frozen, cooked shrimp can be a standby as well, and they are good hot or cold. Pork shoulder steaks, pan-broiled, are a great quick-and-easy option. Frozen pre-formed 100-percent beef hamburgers are a staple around here—they can be cooked from frozen and varied many ways.

Beef steaks I find a little harder. Why? Because I like my steak medium-rare. That calls for a steak at least an inch (2.5 cm) thick, and a steak that big is at least two servings in my mind (and stomach). If you, like me, like your steak pink in the center, you may just have to suffer through leftover steak (see the steak salad recipe on page 71, or make steak and eggs for breakfast). Filet mignon comes in single servings, of course, but it can cause sticker shock. If you like it medium to medium-well, a steak ½ inch (1 cm) thick may serve you well.

However, if you're like me, a diet of nothing but plain meat, poultry, fish, and eggs would pall. I like a variety of flavors and textures and I like to cook!

Here we run up against the simple math of a keto diet: Adding much of anything to our zero-carb staples increases the carb count. Even spices add up. Look at the totals before deciding whether you'll have a side dish.

On the other hand, if you find my portions of meat, poultry, or fish to be skimpy, feel free to bump them up a bit. Zero carbs there.

SOLO JOE

4 ounces (115 g) ground chuck

2 tablespoons (20 g) diced onion

¼ teaspoon minced garlic

½ cup (35 g) sliced mushrooms

1½ cups (45 g) loosely packed spinach leaves

2 eggs

Salt and pepper

1 tablespoon (5 g) grated or shredded Parmesan cheese, plus more to taste (optional)

Yet again I present a version of this quick, tasty, nourishing, inexpensive skillet supper. I know, I know, repetitive of me, but it's the best one-dish skillet meal I know. The recipe calls for two eggs, but you can use just one if you're limiting protein.

1. Put your large, heavy skillet over medium heat and start browning and crumbling the ground beef. When a little fat has cooked out of the beef, throw in the onion, garlic, and mushrooms. Keep cooking until all the pink is gone from the meat, the onions are translucent, and the mushrooms have softened and changed color, 5 to 7 minutes.

2. Add the spinach and stir just until it's wilted.

3. Crack the eggs into a small bowl and beat with a fork. Pour them into the skillet and scramble until set.

4. Add salt and pepper to taste. Serve topped with the Parmesan. Or not. I mean, who's going to argue?

....

1 SERVING with: 481 Calories; 34 g Fat (64.7% calories from fat); 35 g Protein; 6 g Carbohydrate; 2 g Dietary Fiber; 4 g Net Carbs

FIVE-WAY BEEF

So versatile! Start with ground beef seasoned with an Asian accent, then choose a way to serve it.

1. Put your large, heavy skillet over medium heat. Start browning and crumbling the beef while you mince the scallion.

2. As fat cooks out of the beef, add the garlic, sesame oil, ginger, and pepper flakes. Keep browning and crumbling until the pink is gone from the meat, another 5 minutes or so.

3. Add the beef broth and sweetener. Stir it all up, turn the heat down, and let it simmer for 5 minutes.

4. Meanwhile, put a small skillet over medium heat, add the sesame seeds, and stir until they smell toasty—they may even pop a bit—about 3 minutes.

5. Okay, now you have to figure out what to do with your beef. You can:

- Wrap it in lettuce leaves, sprinkling in the sesame seeds.
- Do the same with cabbage leaves instead of lettuce.
- Create a skillet supper by stirring in a cup (43 g) of coleslaw mix and letting it cook another 3 minutes, and serve with the sesame seeds on top.
- Add another tablespoon or two of broth, and serve over shirataki noodles with the sesame seeds on top. I might snip some cilantro on top!
- Or just eat it as-is, with the sesame seeds sprinkled on top.

....

1 SERVING (without the serving suggestions): 546 Calories; 43 g Fat (71.5% calories from fat); 33 g Protein; 5 g Carbohydrate; 1 g Dietary Fiber; 4 g Net Carbs

Add 6 lettuce leaves: 6 Calories; trace Fat (8.6% calories from fat); trace Protein; 1 g Carbohydrate; 1 g Dietary Fiber; 0 g Net Carbs

Add 6 cabbage leaves: 35 Calories; trace Fat (7.9% calories from fat); 2 g Protein; 7 g Carbohydrate; 3 g Dietary Fiber; 4 g Net Carbs

Add 1 cup coleslaw mix: 13 Calories; Trace Fat (0.0% calories from fat); 1 g Protein; 3 g Carbohydrate; 1 g Dietary Fiber; 2 g Net Carbs

Add 1 packet shirataki noodles: 40 Calories; 1 g Fat (22.0% calories from fat); 2 g Protein; 6 g Carbohydrate; 4 g Dietary Fiber; 2 g Net Carbs

6 ounces (170 g) ground beef chuck

1 scallion, or 1½ to 2 tablespoons (9–12 g) scallion from the salad bar

1 tablespoon (10 g) shredded carrot

1 teaspoon minced garlic

1 teaspoon dark sesame oil

½ teaspoon peeled and grated fresh ginger root

1 pinch of red pepper flakes or a squirt of sriracha

2 tablespoons (28 ml) beef broth

1½ teaspoons erythritol blend (see page 14)

2 teaspoons (5 g) sesame seeds

BEEF AND BROCCOLI STIR FRY

I used a chunk of a ½-inch (1 cm) thick chuck steak for this, because I like chuck, it is a good thickness for cutting in strips, and the price was right. But you can use whatever you might have on hand. You can serve this over Miracle Rice (page 17) or cauli-rice (page 53), if you like, but it only adds more carbs. Any meat you don't cut up and stir-fry can simply be cooked for a steak dinner. Or a steak breakfast. And remember the stir-fry rule—have everything ready before you start cooking!

1 cup (150 g) frozen broccoli "cuts," thawed

6 ounces (170 g) beef chuck

2 tablespoons (30 ml) soy sauce

2 teaspoons (10 ml) dry sherry

½ teaspoon minced garlic

½ teaspoon grated fresh ginger root

8 drops plain or English toffee–flavored liquid stevia

6 ounces (170 g) beef chuck

⅛ small onion, sliced

1½ tablespoons (25 ml) MCT oil (see page 16) or 1½ tablespoons (20 g) lard or bland coconut oil, divided

Guar gum or xanthan gum (optional)

Sriracha (optional)

1. To thaw the broccoli, you might give it just a minute or two in a covered bowl in the microwave at about 60 percent power. Drain it before you stir-fry it, or you'll get an awful splatter.

2. In a cereal bowl, stir together the soy sauce, sherry, garlic, ginger root, and stevia to make the sauce.

3. Cut your steak into thin strips about ½ inch (1 cm) wide and 2 inches (5 cm) long. This is easiest to do if it's half-frozen. Put the strips in the sauce and let them marinate for a minute or two.

4. Slice your onion about ⅛ inch (3 mm) thick.

5. Drain the sauce off of your beef strips into a little bowl and reserve. Get as much off the beef as you can—again, you want to avoid splatter.

6. Okay! Put your big skillet over high heat and let it get good and hot. Melt 1 tablespoon of the oil or lard in the skillet. Add the beef and stir-fry until the pink is gone, 4 to 5 minutes. Fish it out and return it to the cereal bowl—don't fret, you'll be heating it again, so germs aren't a concern.

7. Melt the remaining ½ tablespoon of oil or lard in the skillet. Throw in the broccoli and onion, and stir-fry for 3 minutes or so, just until the broccoli becomes brilliantly green and tender-crisp and the onions are just getting soft.

8. Return the beef to the skillet and pour in the reserved sauce. Thicken a tiny bit with your guar or xanthan shaker, if you like. Stir it up and let it cook just 1 to 2 more minutes to let the flavors blend. Shake on a little more soy sauce and/or a squirt of sriracha, if you like.

Note: *About that ginger root: I keep a chunk in a baggie in the freezer and peel it and grate it, frozen, on my microplane grater.*

1 SERVING with: 606 Calories; 46 g Fat (69.5% calories from fat); 33 g Protein; 12 g Carbohydrate; 5 g Dietary Fiber; 7 g Net Carbs

JALAPEÑO CHEESEBURGER

1 jalapeño pepper (or substitute a small banana pepper if you like it milder)

¼ small onion, sliced

1 tablespoon (13 g) bacon grease

Salt and pepper

12 ounces (340 g) ground beef, in 2 patties

4 ounces (115 g) Monterey jack cheese, sliced

A great way to vary simple pre-made 100 percent beef burgers, though you can make your burgers yourself, of course. I made this two servings so as not to leave you with half a pepper. Stash half the jalapeño-onion mixture in a snap-top container in the fridge and have another burger tomorrow.

1. Remove the stem, seeds, and pith from your jalapeño, and thinly slice the rest. Thinly slice your quarter onion, too.

2. Put a medium-size skillet over medium heat and melt the bacon grease. Throw in the jalapeño and onion. Now wash your hands thoroughly right away! Sauté your pepper and onion until limp, 4 to 5 minutes, and add salt and pepper to taste. Remove from the skillet and reserve on a plate.

3. Put your skillet back on the burner and turn the heat up to medium-high. Add the burgers and cook until done to your liking; I use frozen patties and give them about 5 minutes per side.

4. About 2 minutes before your burgers will be done, top them with the cheese, letting it melt as the burgers finish cooking.

5. Top with the jalapeño-onion mixture and serve.

....

2 SERVINGS, each with: 806 Calories; 69 g Fat (77.8% calories from fat); 42 g Protein; 2 g Carbohydrate; Trace Dietary Fiber; 2 g Net Carbs

Note: If you do save half the jalapeño-onion mixture (instead of making a second burger for a companion, or eating two at a sitting), warm it for 20 to 30 seconds in the microwave before putting it on the burger.

SMOKED GOUDA BURGER WITH HORSERADISH BUTTER

6 ounces (170 g) ground beef chuck

Salt and pepper

1-ounce (28 g) slice smoked Gouda cheese

2 teaspoons minced red onion (get a little sliced red onion from the salad bar and mince it)

1½ tablespoons (22 g) Horseradish Butter (page 162)

You can make this with a frozen hamburger patty if you'd rather. I just happened to have some ground chuck on hand. I made the Horseradish Butter while the burger was cooking. I think beer goes better with this than wine. Despite the culture clash, I'd go with Corona Premier—2.6 grams of carbs and gluten-free.

1. Form your ground chuck into a patty ½ inch (1 cm) thick. Salt and pepper on both sides.

2. Put your medium-size skillet over medium-high heat. When it's hot, throw in the burger. Give it 5 to 6 minutes per side, or cook to your liking.

3. About 2 or 3 minutes before the burger is done, top it with the smoked Gouda.

4. Plate the burger, top with the red onion, then the Horseradish Butter.

....

1 SERVING with: 659 Calories; 55 g Fat (75.8% calories from fat); 38 g Protein; 2 g Carbohydrate; Trace Dietary Fiber; 2 g Net Carbs

GRILLED FLANKEN

I was browsing the meat case and there were some lovely flanken-style short ribs, nicely marbled with fat. I had to have them! It was a hot June day, so grilling seemed the obvious choice. These were wonderful—spicy-salty-sweet and tender. This takes starting ahead, but no step takes more than a couple-few minutes.

1. Lay your flanken on a plate. Mix together the steak seasoning and 1 teaspoon of the erythritol blend, and sprinkle both sides of the meat with it. Let that sit while you make the marinade.

2. Mix together the soy sauce, rice vinegar, maple extract, if using, red pepper flakes, ginger, sesame oil, and remaining 2½ teaspoons of the erythritol blend. This is your marinade.

3. Put your flanken in a resealable plastic bag and pour in the marinade. Seal the bag, pressing out the air as you go, and turn the bag to make sure the meat is coated on all sides. Throw them in the fridge and let them sit until suppertime, at least 1 hour or up to 8 hours.

4. Cooking time is here! Get going whatever sort of grill you've got to medium-high heat, or when the coals are well-ashed. When it's ready, drain the flanken and grill just 2 to 3 minutes per side, until done to your liking. No grill? You can broil these close to the flame for 4 to 6 minutes per side. Done!

....

1 SERVING with: 917 Calories; 85 g Fat (83.7% calories from fat); 34 g Protein; 3 g Carbohydrate; Trace Dietary Fiber; 3 g Net Carbs

8 ounces (225 g) flanken-style short ribs

1½ teaspoons steak seasoning (I use Weber Chicago Steak Seasoning; it contains no sugar)

2½ teaspoons (12.5 g) erythritol blend (see page 14), divided

1½ tablespoons (25 ml) soy sauce

1½ teaspoons rice vinegar

1 drop maple extract (optional, but recommended)

1 teaspoon dried red pepper flakes, plus more to taste

⅛ teaspoon ground ginger

½ teaspoon dark sesame oil

BUFFALO DOGS

2 hot dogs, with the lowest carbs you can find

1 tablespoon (14 g) butter

¼ cup (30 g) minced celery

1 tablespoon (10 g) minced scallion

1 teaspoon olive oil

½ teaspoon lemon juice

Salt and pepper

1 tablespoon hot sauce, such as Frank's, Tabasco, or Louisiana brand

1 tablespoon blue cheese salad dressing

Hot dogs are a yes-and-no proposition—they nearly always have at least a little sugar added. On the other hand, if you read labels you can find them with only 2 grams of carb per link, and the fat-to-protein ratio is nearly ideal, plus they're mighty quick to cook.

I borrowed this idea from *Bon Appétit*, though theirs was served on a bun. Since you're not putting your dogs on buns, you'll need to eat them with a fork. If you'd like to up the protein content a little, add crumbled blue cheese.

1. In a medium-size skillet over medium-low heat, start browning the hot dogs in the butter.

2. Meanwhile, throw the celery and scallion in a bowl and add the olive oil and lemon juice. Stir it up, add salt and pepper to taste, and stir again. Don't forget to turn your hot dogs!

3. When your dogs are nicely browned, add the hot sauce to the skillet. It should sizzle and boil. Roll the hot dogs around in it, making sure they're coated and letting the sauce cook down a little. Then plate the hot dogs, scraping all the sauce over them.

4. Top each hot dog with blue cheese dressing and the celery slaw and eat with a fork and knife.

....

1 SERVING with: 587 Calories; 57 g Fat (86.3% calories from fat); 15 g Protein; 5 g Carbohydrate; 1 g Dietary Fiber; 4 g Net Carbs

PICKLE PORK

This simple recipe gives your pork steak a down-home sweet-and-sour tang. Quick, easy, cheap, delicious, keto—what more are you looking for? Please note that while commercially made sugar-free bread-and-butter pickles are not "clean," you can easily turn a jar of organic sour pickles into bread-and-butter pickles, if you like.

Salt and pepper

6 ounces (170 g) pork shoulder steak

1 tablespoon (14 g) lard or bland coconut oil

2 Sugar-Free Bread and Butter Pickle spears, plus ¼ cup (60 ml) pickle juice (page 167)

1½ tablespoons (15 g) minced red onion

3 dashes hot sauce, such as Frank's, Tabasco, or Louisiana

1. Put your skillet over medium-high heat. While it's heating, salt and pepper your pork on both sides.

2. Melt the lard or coconut oil in the skillet, slosh it around to coat, and throw in your pork. Brown it on both sides, about 4 minutes per side.

3. While that's happening, mince your pickles.

4. Okay, the pork is brown on both sides. Transfer it to a plate for a moment. Add the onion to the skillet and sauté for just a minute. Add the pickle juice, chopped pickles, and hot sauce and stir it up.

5. Scraping a space among the veggies, lay your pork steak in the sauce and turn the burner to its lowest setting. Cover the pan and let the pork simmer for 10 minutes. Flip the steak, replace the cover, and give it another 5 to 10 minutes, depending on how thick it is, until the juices run clear and there's no pink around the bone.

6. Plate and top with all the pickle, onion, and pan liquid on top.

....

1 SERVING with: 433 Calories; 36 g Fat (75.5% calories from fat); 22 g Protein; 4 g Carbohydrate; 1 g Dietary Fiber; 3 g Net Carbs

APPLE-GLAZED PORK RIB

I wanted to figure out a rib recipe for you, but there's just no good way to cook one serving of spareribs. Country-style ribs, however, come in convenient single-serving sizes! I had to buy three, but using up the other two wasn't hard.

1. Put your large, heavy skillet over medium heat. Salt and pepper your rib all over.

2. Melt the fat in the skillet and start browning your rib. You'll want to give it about 5 minutes per side, browning it all over.

3. When your rib is nicely golden, transfer it to a plate and add the broth, vinegar, erythritol blend, paprika, mustard, and garlic to the skillet. Stir it all up, scraping up any nice browned bits.

4. Put the rib in the sauce, turning it to coat. Turn the burner to low and partially cover the skillet so the lid sits at a tilt, leaving a small crack for steam to escape. Set the timer for 10 minutes.

5. When the timer beeps, look at your rib. If your sauce is cooking down a little too fast, add a tablespoon of water or extra broth. Flip your rib, replace the cover on the skillet, still leaving it open a crack, and let it cook for another 10 minutes, or until tender.

6. Serve the rib on a plate with all the sauce scraped over it.

....

1 SERVING with: 525 Calories; 43 g Fat (73.4% calories from fat); 29 g Protein; 6 g Carbohydrate; 1 g Dietary Fiber; 5 g Net Carbs

1 country-style pork rib, about 8 ounces (225 g)

Salt and pepper

1 tablespoon (14 g) lard, bacon grease, or bland coconut oil

½ cup (120 ml) chicken broth, plus more as needed

¼ cup (60 ml) cider vinegar

2 teaspoons (10 g) erythritol blend (see page 14)

1 teaspoon smoked paprika, hot or mild as you prefer

½ teaspoon brown mustard

¼ teaspoon minced garlic

PORK AND PEPPERONCINI REFRIGERATOR STEW

7 ounces (195 g) pork shoulder

Salt and pepper

1 tablespoon (15 ml) olive oil

3 pepperoncini peppers (my salad bar has 'em)

2 tablespoons (20 g) diced onion

¼ cup (60 ml) chicken broth, plus more as needed

1 tablespoon dry white wine

1½ teaspoons white balsamic vinegar

2 anchovies

1 teaspoon dried oregano

½ teaspoon minced garlic

⅛ teaspoon dried red pepper flakes

1½ teaspoons minced fresh parsley (optional)

No joke, this stew happened because the chuck roast I thought I had thawed turned out to be pork shoulder. It was already past 7:00, I'd had a glass of wine, and I sure didn't want to run to the grocery store. So I dug through the refrigerator and invented this from what was on hand. It turned out so wonderfully that I will be deliberately thawing pork to make it in the future!

1. Put your large, heavy skillet over medium heat. Cut the pork into cubes. Salt and pepper them lightly.

2. Add the oil to the skillet and slosh it around to coat the bottom. Add the pork cubes and brown them, turning now and then, for about 10 minutes.

3. In the meanwhile, pull the stems out of your pepperoncini and slice them across, about ⅛ inch (3 mm) thick.

4. When the pork cubes have a bit of gold, add the pepperoncini, onion, broth, wine, and vinegar. Bring to a simmer.

5. Add the anchovies and use a fork to mash them into the liquid. Add the oregano, garlic, and red pepper flakes. Give it all a good stir. Partially cover the skillet so that the lid sits at a tilt, leaving a crack for steam to escape. Turn the heat to low and set a timer for 10 minutes.

6. When the timer beeps, stir your stew. If it's looking a little dry, add another couple of tablespoons of broth. Replace the lid, still at a tilt, and simmer for another 10 minutes.

7. Taste and add salt and pepper and dish it up. Should you have parsley on hand, a little snipped on top is nice.

1 SERVING with: 530 Calories; 41 g Fat (71.8% calories from fat); 29 g Protein; 8 g Carbohydrate; 2 g Dietary Fiber; 6 g Net Carbs

PORK IN CAPER SAUCE

I used pork shoulder steak—it's reliably cheap and nice and fatty. But use a pork chop if you prefer, and use a bigger steak if you want more protein—it has no carbs. This is easy to double should you have company.

1. Put a medium-size heavy skillet over medium heat. Salt and pepper your pork steak on both sides.

2. Melt the butter in the skillet, add the pork steak, and brown it on both sides, 3 to 4 minutes per side.

3. Stir the mustard into the broth, then pour it over the pork steak. Cover the skillet and turn the heat to low. Let it simmer for 20 minutes. Use that time to drain and mince your capers.

4. When your pork steak is done through and tender, transfer the steak to a plate and turn off the heat. Stir the sour cream and minced capers into the liquid left in the skillet, and serve over the pork steak.

....

1 SERVING with: 543 Calories; 47 g Fat (77.6% calories from fat); 27 g Protein; 4 g Carbohydrate; Trace Dietary Fiber; 4 g Net Carbs

Salt and pepper

6 ounces (170 g) pork shoulder steak

1 tablespoon (14 g) butter

½ teaspoon brown mustard

¼ cup (60 ml) beef broth or chicken broth

1 teaspoon capers

¼ cup (60 g) sour cream

PORK SATAY

6 ounces (170 g) pork shoulder, cut into 1-inch (2.5 cm) cubes

⅛ small onion

1½ teaspoons MCT oil (see page 16)

½ teaspoon minced garlic

1½ teaspoons soy sauce

⅛ teaspoon lemon juice

⅛ teaspoon ground cumin

⅛ teaspoon ground coriander

⅛ teaspoon ground turmeric

1 drop English toffee–flavored liquid stevia

Fresh cilantro (optional)

Ask your Nice Meat Guys to cut you a 1-inch (2.5 cm) slab from the pork shoulder. If you cut the pork into cubes and put it in the marinade in the morning, or even the night before, cooking this is practically jet-propelled. Peanut Sauce (page 164) makes a nice dip for the pork.

1. Put your pork cubes in a nonreactive bowl—pottery, glass, or stainless steel.

2. Combine the onion, MCT oil, garlic, soy sauce, lemon juice, cumin, coriander, turmeric, and stevia in a compact food processor and run until you have a paste.

3. Scrape the paste into the bowl with the pork cubes and stir until they're all evenly coated. Stash the pork in a covered bowl or resealable bag in the fridge until it's time to cook; the pork should marinate for at least 1 hour and up to 8 hours. If you're going to use bamboo skewers, you might put them in water to soak at this time—they don't need to soak all day, but they can (30 minutes is the minimum amount of soaking time). You'll need two skewers.

4. Come suppertime, put the oven rack 6 to 8 inches (15 cm to 20 cm) under the broiler, and turn the broiler on to preheat. Coat your broiler rack with cooking spray.

5. Thread your pork onto two skewers, either bamboo or metal. Lay them on the broiler pan, and broil, turning a few times for 10 to 12 minutes, until the juices run clear.

6. Serve with a scattering of minced cilantro, if you're a fan.

....

1 SERVING with: 374 Calories; 30 g Fat (72.7% calories from fat); 23 g Protein; 3 g Carbohydrate; Trace Dietary Fiber; 3 g Net Carbs

PORK WITH ORANGE-SAGE SAUCE

Longtime readers will recognize pork shoulder as an old pal. It has so many virtues! It's inexpensive, easy to come by, well-marbled with fat, and super-tasty.

1. Put your large, heavy skillet over medium heat. Salt and pepper your steak on both sides. When the skillet is hot, melt the butter and brown the steak on both sides, 3 to 4 minutes per side. Transfer to a plate and reserve.

2. Add the sherry, chicken broth, lemon juice, and stevia to the skillet. If you're using fresh sage leaves, mince them before adding; if dried, roll them between your fingers to crumble as you add them. Stir everything together.

3. Return the steak to the skillet, flipping it to coat both sides. Turn the heat down to low, cover the skillet, and let it simmer for 10 minutes. Flip the steak, replace the cover, and give it another 10 minutes.

4. Transfer the steak to a serving plate. Your sauce should have cooked down a bit, but turn up the heat and boil it until it cooks down to become slightly syrupy. Thicken a bit with your guar or xanthan shaker, if you like, and add salt and pepper to taste.

5. Serve the steak with the sauce, of course!

....

1 SERVING with: 550 Calories; 42 g Fat (74.1% calories from fat); 30 g Protein; 3 g Carbohydrate; Trace Dietary Fiber; 3 g Net Carbs

Salt and pepper

8 ounces (225 g) pork shoulder steak

1 tablespoon (14 g) butter

2 tablespoons (28 ml) dry sherry

2 tablespoons (28 ml) chicken broth

2 tablespoons (28 ml) lemon juice

12 drops Valencia orange–flavored liquid stevia

6 sage leaves, fresh or dried

Guar gum or xanthan gum (optional)

VAGUELY MEDITERRANEAN LAMB STEAK (OR CHOP)

8 ounces (225 g) lamb leg steak or lamb chops

Salt and pepper

½ teaspoon dried thyme

2 tablespoons (28 ml) olive oil

3 tablespoons (45 ml) beef broth

1 tablespoon (15 g) lemon juice

1 teaspoon minced garlic

1 teaspoon harissa paste (I use Mina brand)

Since That Nice Boy I Married is not a lamb fan, I buy a leg of lamb when it goes on sale, get it sliced into steaks, bag them up, and stash them in the freezer. Perfect for one—but you need the freezer space. If you lack it, go with chops.

1. Sprinkle the lamb on both sides with salt, pepper, and the thyme.

2. Put your skillet over medium heat and let it get hot. Then add the olive oil, slosh it around to coat, and add the lamb. Brown it on both sides, 4 to 5 minutes per side. Transfer the lamb to a plate.

3. Add the beef broth, lemon juice, garlic, and harissa to the skillet and stir it around, scraping up all the nice browned bits. Return the lamb to the skillet, turn the heat to low, and cover the skillet. Let it simmer for 3 minutes, then flip the lamb. Replace the cover and give it another 3 minutes.

4. Plate the lamb. If the sauce hasn't reduced to a syrupy consistency, turn the heat up a little and let the sauce boil for a minute. Pour over the lamb, and it's done.

....

1 SERVING with: 676 Calories; 58 g Fat (77.0% calories from fat); 35 g Protein; 4 g Carbohydrate; Trace Dietary Fiber; 4 g Net Carbs

BOURSIN-AND OLIVE-STUFFED CHICKEN BREAST

My chicken breasts can be quite large, but you can slice the finished dish in two and reheat the leftovers for breakfast the next day. Hey, bacon makes it breakfast food, right? On the other hand, this would make a nice quick company dinner, should you want company. Add a green salad and a bottle of Pinot Grigio, and you're sure to impress.

13 ounces (365 g) boneless, skinless chicken breast

3 tablespoons (45 g) Boursin cheese or other garlic-and-herb spreadable cheese

2 tablespoons (30 g) olive paste (tapenade, olivada, or olive bruschetta spread)

4 slices bacon

1 tablespoon (13 g) bacon grease

1. Slice your chicken breast most of the way through, leaving a "hinge," so you can open it up like a book. Spread the Boursin on one side, then top with the olive spread. Close it up. Wrap the bacon around it, overlapping a bit, covering as much as you can from one end to the other. Fasten with toothpicks as needed.

2. Put your skillet over medium-low heat and throw in the bacon grease. When it's hot, lay your stuffed chicken breast in it. Partially cover with a lid so it sits at a tilt and set a timer for 12 minutes.

3. When the timer beeps, flip carefully, replace the tilted lid, and give it another 12 minutes.

4. Turn on the broiler and arrange the oven rack about 6 inches (15 cm) below it. While it heats, flip the chicken again, replace the tilted lid, and let it cook for another 5 minutes.

5. Almost done! Uncover the chicken and see on which side the bacon is less done—probably the one that is currently down. So flip it and slide it under the broiler. Give it 3 to 5 minutes, until the bacon is crisp all over.

6. That's it! It's easiest to plate this if you cut it in half (crosswise) before lifting it out of the skillet. Store the second serving in an airtight container in the refrigerator and enjoy within 5 days.

....

2 SERVINGS, each with: 470 Calories; 30 g Fat (58.7% calories from fat); 46 g Protein; 2 g Carbohydrate; 0 g Dietary Fiber; 2 g Net Carbs

1 (8-ounce [225 g]) package tofu or traditional shirataki spaghetti or angel hair

¼ cup (60 ml) Peanut Sauce (page 164)

¼ cup (35 g) diced cooked chicken or small, cooked, peeled shrimp

1 scallion, thinly sliced

1 tablespoon (9 g) chopped peanuts

1 tablespoon (1 g) minced cilantro (optional)

Sriracha (optional)

SHIRATAKI WITH CHICKEN (OR SHRIMP) AND PEANUT SAUCE

Having made a peanut sauce to go with the Pork Satay (page 94), I had leftovers on hand just waiting to be used. I combined it with shirataki and the tail end of a rotisserie chicken to make a quick, easy, filling lunch. Even easier, you can grab the chicken and scallions off the salad bar.

1. Prepare the shirataki according to the instructions on page 17.

2. When the noodles are ready, stir in the Peanut Sauce—you can warm it first if you like, or microwave in a bowl for 20 to 30 seconds to help it melt.

3. Stir in the chicken and scallion. Top with the peanuts and the cilantro, if using. Squirt in some sriracha if you're a chile-head!

....

1 SERVING with: 390 Calories; 32 g Fat (71.8% calories from fat); 19 g Protein; 9 g Carbohydrate; 3 g Dietary Fiber; 6 g Net Carbs

CHORIPOLLO

Two ¼ ounce (65 g) fresh
Mexican chorizo

Bacon grease (optional)

4 ounces (115 g) boneless,
skinless chicken breast, cut into
¼-inch (6 mm) strips

½ cup (120 ml) queso dip or
sauce (preferably white queso—
it'll look better)

For twenty-three years I have spent my Thursday nights with my Toastmasters club. Afterward, we usually go out to Casa Brava, a terrific Mexican restaurant in Bloomington, Indiana. This is my riff on a dish they serve, only I can't get chorizo quite as good as theirs. When buying queso sauce or dip, read the labels for the lowest carbs and fewest additives.

1. So simple! Put your big, heavy skillet over medium heat and fry the chorizo until it's done through, about 10 minutes; it will crumble in the process. Scoop it out with a slotted spoon and reserve on a plate.

2. Add the chicken to the skillet, and fry it in the fat left from the chorizo. Add a few teaspoons of bacon grease if you need more fat.

3. When the pink is all gone from the chicken, return the chorizo to the skillet and stir in the queso, and simmer just until heated through. Done!

....

1 SERVING without optional bacon grease: 678 Calories; 48 g Fat (63.4% calories from fat); 58 g Protein; 5 g Carbohydrate; 0 g Dietary Fiber; 5 g Net Carbs

Note: Casa Brava serves Choripollo over rice, but I have them hold the rice and have never missed it. If you like, though, you can serve this over shirataki "rice" or cauli-rice.

GARLIC-PARMESAN CHICKEN

A great one-dish supper, perfect for eating out of a bowl while kicked back in your comfy chair. Use chicken breast, if you prefer; I find the thighs more flavorful.

1. Cut your chicken into 1-inch (2.4 cm) cubes and sprinkle with salt and pepper. If you didn't buy your mushrooms sliced, slice 'em now.

2. Put your medium-size skillet over medium heat. When it's hot, add the olive oil, then throw in the chicken. Sauté for 3 to 4 minutes, stirring often. Throw in the mushrooms and sauté for another 2 to 3 minutes. Break them up into bite-sized pieces with the edge of your spatula as you sauté. Add the spinach and sauté just until it wilts, 1 to 2 minutes.

3. Add the broth, cream, and garlic, and stir it all up. Cover and turn the heat all the way down to its lowest setting. Let it simmer while you prepare the shirataki.

4. Prepare the shirataki according to the instructions on page 17.

5. When the shirataki is fully drained, stir the Parmesan into the chicken and sauce. Pour or spoon the chicken and sauce over the shirataki. Top with a little more Parmesan, if you like.

....

1 SERVING with: 706 Calories; 61 g Fat (78.5% calories from fat); 32 g Protein; 5 g Carbohydrate; 1 g Dietary Fiber; 4 g Net Carbs

6 ounces (170 g) boneless, skinless dark meat chicken (1 good-size thigh, or 2 small ones)

Salt and pepper

2 mushrooms, sliced, or about ½ cup (35 g) sliced mushrooms from the salad bar

2 tablespoons (28 ml) olive oil

1 cup (30 g) loosely packed spinach

¼ cup (60 ml) chicken broth

¼ cup (60 ml) heavy cream

¼ teaspoon minced garlic

1 tablespoon (15 ml) dry white wine (optional)

1 (8-ounce [225 g]) package tofu shirataki spaghetti or fettuccine

2 tablespoons (10 g) grated Parmesan cheese, plus more to serve

1 (8-ounce [225 g]) package tofu shirataki—spaghetti, fettuccine, or angel hair–style

6 ounces (170 g) boneless, skinless dark meat chicken (1 good-size thigh, or 2 small ones)

3 tablespoons (45 ml) olive oil

1 teaspoon minced garlic

⅛ teaspoon dried red pepper flakes

1 cup (67 g) lightly packed stemmed and chopped kale

1½ teaspoons lemon juice

½ teaspoon finely grated lemon zest

Salt and pepper

2 tablespoons (10 g) grated or shredded Parmesan cheese

PASTA WITH LEMON-KALE CHICKEN

Quick and easy, and so good! Many thanks to my friend and crack recipe tester Julie McIntosh for turning me on to this idea. I buy just enough kale for the recipe from the grocery store salad bar—no leftovers! Use boneless, skinless chicken breast, if you prefer.

1. First, prepare the shirataki according to the instructions on page 17.

2. While the noodles are in the microwave, cut your chicken into bite-sized cubes.

3. Put your big, heavy skillet over medium-high heat, and add the olive oil. Throw in the chicken, garlic, and red pepper flakes, and sauté for about 5 minutes, stirring often. When the pink is gone from the chicken, throw in the kale and sauté until just wilted, 1 to 2 minutes.

4. Stir in the lemon juice and zest, then add the shirataki and toss until everything is friendly. Add salt and pepper to taste.

5. Pile it on a plate or in a bowl, top with the Parmesan, and dig in.

....

1 SERVING with: 625 Calories; 53 g Fat (74.9% calories from fat); 31 g Protein; 9 g Carbohydrate; 2 g Dietary Fiber; 7 g Net Carbs

BUTTER-LEMON FISH

I make this with a trout fillet, but I can't think of a variety of fish it wouldn't work with. Quick, easy, and it doesn't even dirty up a pan. The foil keeps the fish moist while letting it sear bit.

6 ounces (170 g) fish fillet

Salt and pepper

2 tablespoons (28 g) butter

½ lemon

1. Tear off a sheet of aluminum foil about 12 inches (30 cm) long and lay it on the counter. Put your fish on it and sprinkle with salt and pepper.

2. Cut your butter into six pats. Slice your half-lemon paper thin, flicking out the seeds.

3. Lay three butter pats in a row next to the fish fillet, then lay three lemon slices over them. Flip the fish over onto the lemon slices. Sprinkle salt and pepper on the other side of the fish and lay the rest of the lemon slices along the fish. Top that with the rest of the butter. Fold the foil up over the fish and fold down to make a seam, then fold in the ends, making an airtight packet.

4. Put a skillet big enough for the packet over medium heat. When it's good and hot, put the packet in, seam side down. Use a spatula to press it flat against the skillet. The cooking time will depend a bit on the thickness of your fish—a trout fillet a little more than ½ inch (1 cm) thick took 7 minutes on the side with the seam, then another 5 minutes on the other side. Why the difference? Because the extra foil on the seam side slows the heat transfer a little.

5. Eat your fish right out of the packet!

....

1 SERVING with: 349 Calories; 24 g Fat (61.6% calories from fat); 31 g Protein; 3 g Carbohydrate; Trace Dietary Fiber; 3 g Net Carbs

LIME SALMON WITH LIME-CHIPOTLE CREMA

6 ounces (170 g) salmon fillet

1 tablespoon (15 ml) lime juice, divided

Salt and pepper

1 tablespoon (15 ml) olive oil

1 tablespoon (15 g) sour cream

1 teaspoon chipotle hot sauce, or more to taste

¼ teaspoon minced garlic

Minced fresh cilantro (optional)

Okay, it's really sour cream, not Mexican crema; where I live, authentic crema is scarce. Still yummy, and ups the fat percentage. Add a leafy green salad with vinaigrette on the side.

1. Rub 1 teaspoon of the lime juice onto both sides of your salmon. Sprinkle salt and pepper all over.

2. Coat your medium-size skillet with cooking spray and put it over medium heat. When the skillet is hot, add the oil and slosh it around to coat, then throw in the salmon. Depending on how thick your fillet is, cook for 3 to 4 minutes per side, until the fish flakes easily.

3. Make the crema while the salmon cooks. Stir together the sour cream with the remaining 2 teaspoons lime juice, the hot sauce, and the garlic. Taste and add a little salt and pepper, if you like.

4. Need I explain? Plate the fish, top with the crema. If you like cilantro, it is nice sprinkled on top, but it's not essential, by any means.

....

1 SERVING with: 353 Calories; 22 g Fat (57.8% calories from fat); 34 g Protein; 2 g Carbohydrate; Trace Dietary Fiber; 2 g Net Carbs

CRAB CAKES WITH ORANGE SAUCE

½ cup (28 g) pork rind crumbs, divided

1 egg, lightly beaten

2 tablespoons (28 g) mayonnaise

2 tablespoons (8 g) minced fresh parsley

1 tablespoon (10 g) minced onion

½ teaspoon minced garlic

¼ teaspoon salt or Vege-Sal

⅛ teaspoon dry mustard

3 dashes of hot sauce

8 ounces (226 g) fresh or pasteurized lump crabmeat

1 shallot, minced

2 tablespoons (28 g) butter

¼ cup (60 ml) white balsamic vinegar

¼ cup (60 ml) lemon juice

2 tablespoons (30 ml) dry white wine

1 tablespoon (15 g) erythritol blend (see page 14)

½ teaspoon orange extract

3 tablespoons (45 ml) MCT or bland coconut oil (see page 16)

2 tablespoons (30 ml) heavy cream

This is an instance where the main ingredient, the crab, is only available in one size: 8 ounces, which makes two servings. If it's just you, store the cooked cakes and sauce separately in airtight containers in the refrigerator and have crab cakes again tomorrow. Warm the crab cakes in a little oil in a skillet, just like you cooked them. The microwave will reheat the sauce, but it won't do for the crab cakes—they'll wind up with a soggy surface.

1. In a mixing bowl, combine 6 tablespoons (21 g) of the pork rind crumbs with the egg, mayonnaise, parsley, onion, garlic, salt, dry mustard, and hot sauce. Whisk it all up until everything is evenly distributed.

2. Add the crab and stir it in gently, taking care to maintain some chunks of crab. Form into four patties, each about 2½ inches (6 cm) across and ½ inch (1 cm) thick, pressing together firmly; they'll be a bit crumbly.

3. Scatter the remaining 2 tablespoons (7 g) pork rind crumbs on a plate and gently press the crab cakes in it. Put them on a plate and refrigerate while you make the sauce.

4. Mince the shallot. In a small saucepan over medium-low heat, melt the butter and sauté the shallot for 2 to 3 minutes, until softened a little. Add the balsamic vinegar, lemon juice, wine, sweetener, and orange extract. Bring to a simmer and let it cook down by about half, about 10 minutes.

5. While the sauce is cooking down, give your large, heavy skillet a squirt of cooking spray and put it over medium heat. When your skillet is hot, add the oil and slosh it around, then put in the crab cakes. Cook for about 7 minutes per side, until golden.

6. Whisk the cream into the sauce. Plate the cakes. Serve the sauce in small dishes on the side.

....

2 SERVINGS, each with: 681 Calories; 57 g Fat (74.8% calories from fat); 36 g Protein; 7 g Carbohydrate; Trace Dietary Fiber; 7 g Net Carbs

TROUT IN TARRAGON CREAM

Yet again, fish yields a fast meal that would impress a restaurant critic. I'd call for fresh tarragon, but it's unlikely you'd use it up before it became sad and wilted. I used dried and That Nice Boy I Married licked the plate clean.

1. Give your skillet a shot of cooking spray and put it over medium heat. While it heats up, salt and pepper the trout on both sides.

2. Cooking time! Throw the butter into the hot skillet, let it melt, and slosh it around. Lay the trout fillet in the butter and give it 3 to 4 minutes on each side, until the flesh flakes easily. Transfer to a plate.

3. Add the minced shallot to the skillet and sauté for a minute or two. Add the parsley, tarragon, wine, and heavy cream. Cook for 2 to 3 minutes, until it's thickened a little.

4. Turn the heat down to low. Return the trout to the skillet, let it simmer for just a minute, then plate, pouring the sauce over it. Garnish with a little more parsley if you're taking photos for Instagram.

....

1 SERVING with: 677 Calories; 52 g Fat (73.5% calories from fat); 38 g Protein; 5 g Carbohydrate; Trace Dietary Fiber; 5 g Net Carbs

Note: *Shallots are red, teardrop-shaped relatives of onions and garlic. They usually come with two halves inside the papery skin. You're only using one of those halves; save the other for another recipe—or to make this again!*

Salt and pepper

6 ounces (170 g) trout fillet

1 tablespoon (14 g) butter

1 shallot, minced

1 teaspoon minced fresh parsley, plus more to garnish

½ teaspoon dried tarragon

¼ cup (60 ml) dry white wine

⅓ cup (80 ml) heavy cream

SCALLOPS WITH BROWNED BUTTER, BACON, AND ASPARAGUS

This is quick and easy, yet satisfyingly "gourmet." Tell me you wouldn't order this at a restaurant for vastly more money!

1 tablespoon (8 g) bacon bits

6 sea scallops

Salt and pepper

2 tablespoons (28 g) butter

4 asparagus spears

1 teaspoon lemon juice

2 teaspoons (10 ml) chicken broth or seafood stock

1. Give your skillet a squirt of cooking spray and put it over medium heat. While it's heating, spread your bacon bits on a small plate and microwave them for 20 to 30 seconds to refresh.

2. Pat the scallops dry with paper towels and sprinkle them lightly on both sides with salt and pepper.

3. Melt the butter in the skillet over medium heat and lay the scallops in it. Cook them for 4 to 5 minutes per side, until lightly seared on the surface and white clear through.

4. Snap the ends off the asparagus where they want to break naturally. Put the spears on a plate, add just ½ teaspoon of water, cover with plastic wrap or another plate, inverted, and microwave on High for 2 minutes. (If you are multitasking, don't forget to flip your scallops!)

5. As soon as your asparagus is done, uncover it. When your scallops are browned on both sides, arrange them artfully on the asparagus spears.

6. The butter in the skillet should have browned while your scallops were cooking. Add the lemon juice and broth to the skillet and stir it around, dissolving all the yummy browned stuff. Cook for just a minute, then pour over the scallops and asparagus. Sprinkle the bacon on top, pour yourself a glass of dry white wine, and sigh happily.

....

1 SERVING with: 300 Calories; 25 g Fat (73.2% calories from fat); 14 g Protein; 6 g Carbohydrate; 2 g Dietary Fiber; 4 g Net Carbs

SHERRY-GLAZED SHRIMP

3 tablespoons (42 g) butter

6 ounces (170 g) large shrimp, peeled and veined

2 tablespoons (28 ml) dry sherry

2 teaspoons lemon juice

1 pinch of cayenne

With a dish this delicious, you're going to be your own favorite dinner date. Should you choose to share, it's no trouble to double this, and it'll impress the heck out of your lucky guest. This goes fast! Have the shrimp peeled, the butter out, and the sherry, lemon juice, and cayenne measured into a small dish by the stove before you start cooking.

1. Put your skillet over medium-high heat and melt the butter. Throw in the shrimp and sauté, stirring often, for 3 minutes.

2. Add the sherry, lemon juice, and cayenne and keep stirring until it has reduced to just a glaze on the shrimp.

3. Serve with dry white wine or a sip of sherry and a very smug expression.

....

1 SERVING with: 473 Calories; 36 g Fat (73.0% calories from fat); 28 g Protein; 1 g Carbohydrate; Trace Dietary Fiber; 1 g Net Carbs

SCALLOP SHIRATAKI WITH SUN-DRIED TOMATOES AND PINE NUTS

Wow. Just…wow. You're going to want to post pictures of this on Instagram to make your friends jealous.

1. Prepare the shirataki according to the instructions on page 17.

2. Pat your scallops dry with paper towels and cut them in half horizontally.

3. Put a medium-size skillet over medium-low heat. Add the pine nuts and stir them until they're golden, 4 to 5 minutes. Transfer them to a plate.

4. Add the olive oil to the skillet and let it get hot. Salt and pepper the scallops lightly, put them in the oil, and let them sear—3 to 4 minutes per side. Add the garlic, parsley, red pepper flakes, and that olive oil from the sun-dried tomatoes. Stir briefly.

5. Scrape the scallops and all the stuff from the pan over the shirataki and add the chopped sun-dried tomatoes. Toss, then top with the Parmesan and pine nuts.

....

1 SERVING with: 411 Calories; 36 g Fat (78.0% calories from fat); 17 g Protein; 6 g Carbohydrate; 1 g Dietary Fiber; 5 g Net Carbs

Note: If you can get teeny bay scallops instead of the larger sea scallops, so much the better, and you don't need to halve 'em. Use 12 to 18.

1 (8-ounce [225 g]) package tofu shirataki spaghetti or fettuccine

6 sea scallops

1½ tablespoons (10 g) chopped oil-packed sun-dried tomatoes, plus 2 teaspoons (10 ml) of the oil

1 tablespoon (9 g) pine nuts

Salt and pepper

2 tablespoons (28 ml) olive oil

½ teaspoon minced garlic

1 tablespoon (4 g) minced fresh parsley

1 pinch of red pepper flakes

2 tablespoons (10 g) grated Parmesan cheese

CHAPTER 6

SNACKS AND SWEETS

There's an issue with snacks on a keto diet: If you're eating more than plain meat for meals, you don't have a lot of wiggle room left in your carb allowance for more. Too, you shouldn't need many snacks—you'll feel full! One of the clearest signs you're in ketosis is a dramatically reduced appetite. Make use of it to stretch out the time between meals. Think of these recipes more as light meals.

You no doubt know that pork rinds are the ultimate keto snack. Nuts, too, fit into a keto plan. Keep in mind that the lowest carb/highest fat nuts are macadamias, pecans, and walnuts. Also keep in mind that it's easy to overeat nuts.

Regarding sweets: I learned from Mary Vernon, MD, a diabetologist and bariatric physician, that we have tastebuds in our small intestines, just like the tissue on our tongues. When they sense anything sweet, whether it's

from sugar, artificial sweeteners, stevia, monk fruit, whatever, they signal the body to release a little insulin to deal with the expected rise in blood sugar. If that rise doesn't come, the body won't release more, but there will still have been that little bump in insulin. All sweets, even the best of them, come at that cost.

On the other hand, for many people the idea of never eating anything sweet again is daunting and will cause them to walk away from the keto diet. That would be a darned shame. You'll find plenty to satisfy your sweet tooth here. Just don't be surprised if your taste for sweets diminishes over time.

Oh, and the simplest sweet keto treat is a couple of squares of 85 percent dark chocolate—1 ounce (28 g) has 11 grams of carb, 4 of them from fiber, for a net carb count of 7 grams. But you have to be able to quit at 1 ounce. Know thyself.

ORANGE-PEPPER PECANS

1 teaspoon lemon juice

¼ teaspoon orange extract

1 tablespoon (15 ml) MCT oil (see page 16)

1 cup (110 g) pecans

1 tablespoon (15 g) erythritol blend (see page 14)

Rounded ¼ teaspoon pepper, or a scant ½ teaspoon

¼ teaspoon salt, or to taste

Repeat after me: This recipe makes four servings. Four servings. Four servings. All four of them for you, of course. If this recipe isn't amazing enough for you on its own, try dipping the pecans in the peanut butter dip from page 121.

1. In a small dish, combine the lemon juice and orange extract. Have this by the stove.

2. Put your big, heavy skillet over medium heat. Add the MCT oil and pecans. Stir to coat, then spread them evenly over the bottom of the skillet. Let them cook for 4 to 5 minutes, stirring and flipping every 60 seconds, until they smell toasty and begin to brown.

3. Pour in the lemon juice and orange extract, then sprinkle the erythritol blend over it all. Stir it up. Sprinkle the pepper and salt over the pecans and keep stirring until the liquid and erythritol blend are reduced to a syrup on the pecans. Transfer to a plate to cool and store in a snap-top container.

....

4 SERVINGS, each with: 211 Calories; 22 g Fat (87.1% calories from fat); 2 g Protein; 5 g Carbohydrate; 2 g Dietary Fiber; 3 g Net Carbs

VANILLA-GLAZED WALNUTS

1 tablespoon (14 g) butter

1 cup (120 g) walnuts

1½ teaspoons vanilla extract

2 tablespoons (30 g) erythritol blend (see page 14)

Salt

Is it a snack or a sweet? Both! It's a tasty nibble.

1. Put your large, heavy skillet over medium-low heat, melt the butter, and stir in the walnuts. Sauté them, stirring and turning them over every minute or so, until they are a little brown, 5 to 6 minutes.

2. Stir in the vanilla and erythritol blend and keep stirring until the nuts are coated. Salt lightly.

3. Cool and store in a tightly lidded container at room temperature for the roughly 48 hours it takes you to eat the whole batch.

....

4 SERVINGS, each with: 220 Calories; 21 g Fat (79.6% calories from fat); 8 g Protein; 4 g Carbohydrate; 2 g Dietary Fiber; 2 g Net Carbs

PEANUT BUTTER DIP OR SPREAD

Perfect for a late-night munchy attack! Spread it on pork rinds, and it will satisfy both the sweet and salty demons. Or make yourself some Magic Cheese Crackers (page 125) and spread with this dip: a nice flavor contrast! So quick and easy, you can make it during the recap of the previous episode. And you don't have to share the dip or the remote.

3 tablespoons (18 g) whipped cream cheese

1 tablespoon (16 g) natural peanut butter, smooth or chunky

24 drops English toffee–flavored liquid stevia

½ teaspoon vanilla extract

1 pinch of salt (or 2 pinches, if your peanut butter isn't salted)

Measure everything into a small bowl. Mix well with a fork.

....

1 SERVING with: 204 Calories; 18 g Fat (80. 3% calories from fat); 5 g Protein; 5 g Carbohydrate; 1 g Dietary Fiber; 4 g Net Carbs

ARTICHOKE-SPINACH-OLIVE BEEF ROLLUPS

2 ounces (55 g) deli roast beef, cut in 3 slices (ask the deli guys to slice it fairly thick)

3 tablespoons (34 g) Alouette brand Spinach and Artichoke Spreadable Cheese (or a similar product)

2 tablespoons (30 g) olive paste, tapenade, or olivada, or olive bruschetta spread

½ cup (15 g) loosely packed baby spinach

Salt and pepper

This makes for a substantial snack or a light lunch in hot weather. If you want to be fancy, you can cut the rolls into slices and lay them in pretty little whirligigs on a plate. Or just eat 'em.

Find the olive paste, tapenade, or olivada with the jarred olives at your favorite grocery store or specialty food store.

1. Lay a slice of deli roast beef on a plate. Spread with 1 tablespoon of the Alouette Spinach and Artichoke Spreadable Cheese. Arrange the olive spread along one of the short ends of the slice of beef, then lay a single layer of spinach leaves over the whole thing.

2. Roll up, starting at the end with the olive spread so it is in the center. Sprinkle lightly with salt and pepper.

3. Repeat with the remaining ingredients, making three rolls, total.

....

1 SERVING with: 297 Calories; 22 g Fat (63.4% calories from fat); 19 g Protein; 9 g Carbohydrate; Trace Dietary Fiber; 9 g Net Carbs

2 tablespoons (18 g) pine nuts

½ roasted red pepper, drained

2 ounces (55 g) deli roast beef, cut in 3 slices (ask the deli guys to slice it fairly thick)

3 tablespoons (45 g) Boursin cheese

ROASTED RED PEPPER AND PINE NUT BEEF ROLLUPS

Having had such a good time with the Artichoke-Spinach-Olive Beef Rollups, I decided to try these. So glad I did! About the peppers: They're not immortal, even in the refrigerator, so if you're not likely to use up a whole jar, look for them at the antipasto bar at your grocery store; mine carries them. Then you can buy just one or two at a time.

1. Put a small skillet over medium-low heat and stir the pine nuts in it until they're lightly golden, 4 to 5 minutes. Remove from the heat.

2. Cut your half-roasted red pepper into three long strips.

3. Lay a slice of roast beef on a plate. Spread a tablespoon of Boursin on it. Lay a strip of red pepper along one end, and sprinkle pine nuts alongside it. Roll the whole thing up with the red pepper and pine nuts in the center.

4. Repeat with the remaining ingredients.

....

1 SERVING with: 434 Calories; 31 g Fat (63.2% calories from fat); 31 g Protein; 10 g Carbohydrate; 1 g Dietary Fiber; 9 g Net Carbs

MAGIC CHEESE CRACKERS

These are the best cure for your crunchy-salty cravings and you can make 'em one at a time. You can buy these at the grocery store, but they're so easy to make and so good fresh, why bother? Plus, you can make them with any kind of hard cheese you like—Parmesan, Cheddar, Gouda, you name it. Processed American singles work remarkably well.

One caveat: Don't use packaged shredded cheese with additives. It's not that cellulose scares me; it just makes an inferior cracker.

About ⅔ ounce (19 g) cheese, sliced or shredded

1. The easiest way to do this is to grab a piece of baking parchment about the size of a salad plate, but you can use the actual salad plate instead if you like. If you do, coat it with cooking spray. Lay your cheese on it (if you're using shredded, make a slightly flattened heap).

2. Microwave until crisp. In my microwave, 75 seconds on High is perfect for a slice of American cheese, which weighs just under ¾ ounce (21 g). Let cool until you can touch it without burning yourself, and you're done!

....

1 SERVING with: 76 Calories; 6 g Fat (74.0% calories from fat); 5 g Protein; trace Carbohydrate; 0g Dietary Fiber; Trace Net Carbs

HOT, BUTTERY TOAST MIX

1 cup (55 g) plus 2 tablespoons (14 g) almond meal

4 teaspoons (18 g) baking powder

¾ teaspoon salt

¼ cup (27 g) powdered egg whites

1½ teaspoons nutritional yeast flakes

¾ teaspoon guar gum or xanthan gum

I did a version of this for *The New 500 Low-Carb Recipes*, but it called for a fresh egg white. I know very few people who want to separate an egg on a busy morning. I decided to come up with a mix, to make toast a weekday morning option.

Just mix everything together, making sure there are no lumps of anything and that all the ingredients are evenly distributed. Keep in a snap-top container. If you're going to use it up within a week or so, you can skip refrigeration, but if you're likely to keep it longer, in the fridge it goes.

....

6 SERVINGS, each with: 148 Calories; 5 g Fat (28.4% calories from fat); 19 g Protein; 9 g Carbohydrate; Trace Dietary Fiber; 9 g Net Carb

Note: *I used to be able to buy powdered egg whites in the baking aisle of any local grocery store, but they seem to have gone away. Now I order mine from Amazon. So long as they're dry, they're shelf-stable. Do not confuse these with powdered whole eggs!*

HOT, BUTTERY TOAST MADE FROM MIX

You want toast with your eggs? Something to spread a little peanut butter on? Maybe melt some cheese? Or have gloriously buttery toast with your tea? You've got it. And just enough for one!

2 tablespoons (28 g) butter, divided

¼ cup (20 g) Hot, Buttery Toast Mix (page 126)

2 tablespoons (30 ml) water

1. Coat a mug or small custard cup with nonstick cooking spray. Put 1½ tablespoons of the butter in it, and microwave it on High for 30 to 40 seconds, until the butter melts.

2. Add your Hot, Buttery Toast Mix and the water, and whisk thoroughly. You don't want any pockets of dry stuff. You might even run a rubber scraper around the edges.

3. Microwave for 90 to 100 seconds on High, until cooked through. Using oven mitts, remove from the microwave and tip it out onto a plate or cutting board. Do not expect your bread to rise to fill the mug —it will be roughly the thickness of two slices of bread. It will look uninspiring. Panic not.

4. When the bread has cooled enough to handle, slice crosswise into two rounds.

5. Melt the remaining butter in a medium-size skillet over medium heat. Fry your bread rounds on both sides until golden and crunchy, 2 to 3 minutes per side.

....

1 SERVING with: 351 Calories; 28 g Fat (69.4% calories from fat); 19 g Protein; 9 g Carbohydrate; Trace Dietary Fiber; 9 g Net Carbs

CHOCOLATE-PEANUT BUTTER NO-BAKES

You can throw these together in 5 minutes, though chilling takes a little longer. Just the thing when you want a nibble of something sweet. If you want to halve this, go ahead, but why wouldn't you want an extra waiting in the fridge? Make these with almond butter instead of peanut butter, if you prefer.

1. Measure the peanut butter and butter into a microwaveable bowl and microwave on High for just 20 seconds, to soften.

2. Add the coconut, cocoa powder, stevia, and vanilla and stir it up well.

3. Line a small plate with waxed paper or baking parchment and spoon the mixture into two rounds, spreading with the back of the spoon as needed.

4. Chill until firm, about 30 minutes. That's it! Store the extra in a snap-top container in the refrigerator for up to 5 days.

....

2 SERVINGS, each with: 158 Calories; 14 g Fat (77.2% calories from fat); 4 g Protein; 5 g Carbohydrate; 2 g Dietary Fiber; 3 g Net Carbs

2 tablespoons (32 g) natural peanut butter, chunky or smooth

2 teaspoons (9 g) butter

3 tablespoons (15 g) shredded coconut

2 teaspoons (4 g) unsweetened cocoa powder

12 drops English toffee–flavored liquid stevia

⅛ teaspoon vanilla extract

VANILLA CHIA PUD

¼ cup (60 ml) heavy cream

¼ cup (60 ml) unsweetened pourable coconut milk

2 tablespoons (22 g) chia seeds

¼ teaspoon vanilla extract

¼ teaspoon vanilla-flavored liquid stevia, or to taste

Unlike starchy puddings, this requires no cooking! Just stir it up and let it sit for 15 minutes or overnight. Whatever. If you don't like stevia, use liquid sucralose or monk fruit to equal ¼ cup (50 g) sugar in sweetness, and increase the vanilla to 1 teaspoon. If you like, make this in a snap-top container and refrigerate overnight, or even for a couple-few days. I like to warm it a little before eating, though—just to room temperature. Or warm it a little more, and stir in a few Lily's sugar-free chocolate chips.

Combine everything in a medium-size bowl and stir it up. Let it sit for at least 15 minutes to thicken. Done!

....

1 SERVING with: 363 Calories; 32 g Fat (77.7% calories from fat); 6 g Protein; 15 g Carbohydrate; 10 g Dietary Fiber; 5 g Net Carbs

PEANUT BUTTER CHIA PUD

¼ cup (60 ml) heavy cream

¼ cup (60 ml) unsweetened pourable coconut milk

2 tablespoons (22 g) chia seeds

1 tablespoon (16 g) natural peanut butter

¼ teaspoon English toffee–flavored liquid stevia

1 pinch of salt

Same basic chia mixture as the vanilla pudding, but with great peanutty flavor! Use smooth or chunky peanut butter, as you prefer. I made this ahead and refrigerated it. It was very stiff when chilled, but 20 seconds in the microwave softened it up to a lovely texture. If you want to microwave it until it's actually warm, you can stir in a few sugar-free chocolate chips (Lily's makes these), or a little chopped 85 percent dark chocolate. Yum. Or swirl in a spoonful of Polaner Sugar-Free Preserves—the lowest carb preserves I've found—for PB&J Pudding.

1. In a bowl, combine the cream, coconut milk, and chia seeds, stirring well. Let this sit for at least 15 minutes, and overnight in the fridge isn't crazy.

2. Put your peanut butter in a small dish—I use a custard cup—and microwave for just 20 seconds to soften. Stir into the pudding, along with the stevia and salt. Done!

....

1 SERVING with: 452 Calories; 40 g Fat (76.8% calories from fat); 9 g Protein; 18 g Carbohydrate; 11 g Dietary Fiber; 7 g Net Carbs.

PICAYUNE PECAN PUDDING

Pecan pie filling without the crust; another adaptation from my idol, Peg Bracken. Why two servings? Did you really want half an egg left over? Just have the second serving tomorrow night. If you're feeling fancy, save a couple of pecan halves, and place one decoratively on top of each pudding before baking.

1. Preheat the oven to 300°F (150°C). Coat 2 custard cups with cooking spray.

2. Put all the ingredients in your food processor or blender. Pulse the food processor or run the blender until the pecans are chopped to a medium consistency.

3. Divide the mixture into the prepared custard cups. Place them in a baking pan or pie plate. Place in the oven, then pour water around the custard cups to within ½ inch (1 cm) of the rim.

4. Bake for 25 minutes, then turn off the oven and let the pudding sit in the water bath in the oven until everything's cooled enough to handle. Chill before serving. Store the extra serving in the refrigerator for up to 1 week.

....
2 SERVINGS, each with: 305 Calories; 30 g Fat (85.6% calories from fat); 5 g Protein; 6 g Carbohydrate; 2 g Dietary Fiber; 4 g Net Carbs

1 egg

2 tablespoons (30 ml) heavy cream

1 teaspoon sherry

20 drops liquid English toffee–flavored stevia

⅛ teaspoon salt

2 tablespoons (30 g) erythritol blend (see page 14)

½ teaspoon vanilla extract

2 teaspoons (9 g) butter

½ cup pecans

GINGERBREAD MUFFIN-IN-A-MINUTE

I debated over whether this was one or two servings. It really is pretty big. I'm happy splitting it with That Nice Boy I Married, but you could save half for later. Or you could just nom the whole thing down and not eat again for six hours or so. I spread mine with lots of whipped cream cheese, but feel free to make whipped cream, if you like.

1 teaspoon coconut oil, MCT oil (see page 16), or butter

3 tablespoons (21 g) almond meal

2 tablespoons (16 g) vanilla whey protein powder

2–3 tablespoons (30–45 g) erythritol blend (see page 14)

2 teaspoons ground ginger

1 teaspoon ground cinnamon

½ teaspoon baking powder

1 pinch of salt

1 egg

18 drops English toffee–flavored liquid stevia

1. Coat a good, big mug with nonstick cooking spray. Put the oil or butter in it and, if you're using a solid fat, microwave it on High for 20 seconds to melt.

2. Grab a cereal bowl and a sifter. Put your almond meal, whey protein powder, erythritol blend, ginger, cinnamon, baking powder, and salt into the sifter and sift into the cereal bowl, thus assuring equal distribution.

3. Grab your mug with the oil in it. Crack the egg into it and add the liquid stevia. Whisk the two together.

4. Now add the dry ingredients and whisk them in, making sure there are no pockets of dry stuff—running a rubber scraper around the sides helps here.

5. When the batter is smooth, microwave on High for 90 seconds. It will rise fairly spectacularly over the rim of the mug, but will deflate a bit as it cools.

6. When you can handle it, tip it out onto a plate and split into two rounds. Store the extra serving in a snap-top container at room temperature for a few days.

....

2 SERVINGS, each with: 170 Calories; 8 g Fat (40.1% calories from fat); 19 g Protein; 8 g Carbohydrate; 1 g Dietary Fiber; 7 g Net Carbs

FUDGY CHOCOLATE ALMOST PUDDING CAKE IN A MUG

2 tablespoons (28 g) butter

2 tablespoons (10 g) cocoa powder

1½ tablespoons (22 g) erythritol blend (see page 14)

1 pinch of salt

1 egg yolk

2 tablespoons (30 ml) heavy cream

¼ teaspoon vanilla extract

12 pieces Lily's sugar-free chocolate chips (optional)

I was shooting for a lava cake, pudding cake, or something of the sort. This isn't really either, but it's dense, moist, and intensely chocolatey, with both a fudgy and pudding-like thing going on. Too good to skip!

Don't expect this to rise much. It has no leavening, after all. It'll be maybe 2 inches high (5 cm). That's why it's dense and moist! If you are into such things, you can serve this with a scoop of low-carb vanilla ice cream or with whipped cream.

1. Coat a mug with cooking spray. Put the butter in it and microwave for 30 seconds to melt it.

2. Add the cocoa powder, erythritol, salt, egg yolk, heavy cream, and vanilla and use a whisk or a fork to stir it all up until you have a uniform batter. If you're using the chips, sprinkle them over the top and let them sink in a bit.

3. Microwave on High for 90 seconds.

4. Let it cool until you can handle it safely, then tip it out onto a plate.

....

1 SERVING with: 404 Calories; 41 g Fat (86.8% calories from fat); 6 g Protein; 8 g Carbohydrate; 4 g Dietary Fiber; 4 g Net Carbs

CHOCOLATE CHIP-
BUTTERSCOTCH BARS

I got the idea of baking a small batch of cookie bars in a loaf pan from a small-batch baking book. They said it made 4 bars. I found those bars awfully big, so I cut them in half, but do as you please. Who's going to quarrel?

1. Preheat the oven to 325°F (170°C). Line a 9- x 5-inch (23 x 13 cm) loaf pan with nonstick foil along the bottom and about 1 inch (2.5 cm) up the sides.

2. In a medium-size mixing bowl, combine the almond meal, vanilla whey protein, erythritol, baking powder, and salt. Use a whisk to stir this all together to make sure it's equally distributed.

3. Melt the butter, then add it along with the egg, vanilla, and molasses. Stir it all together very well. The dough will be quite stiff. Stir in the chocolate chips and pecans. Spread or press the dough into the prepared loaf pan.

4. Bake for 20 to 25 minutes, until golden and just firm. Let cool in the pan before slicing.

....

8 SERVINGS, each with: 138 Calories; 10 g Fat (61.4% calories from fat); 9 g Protein; 5 g Carbohydrate; 1 g Dietary Fiber; 4 g Net Carbs

¼ cup (28 g) almond meal

¼ cup (32 g) vanilla whey protein powder

¼ cup (60 g) erythritol blend (see page 14)

¼ teaspoon baking powder

⅛ teaspoon salt

2 tablespoons (28 g) butter, melted

1 egg

½ teaspoon vanilla extract

⅛ teaspoon molasses

⅓ cup (58 g) Lily's sugar-free chocolate chips

⅓ cup (37 g) chopped pecans

CHAPTER 7

DRINKABLES

Surely you know that water is keto-friendly. So are coffee and tea, black or green, so long as you don't lace them with sugar. (It is stunning the degree to which my parents' cup of joe has become a huge serving of liquid candy.) Sparkling water is also great.

Diet soda is better than the sugary stuff, but keep in mind that anything sweet, sugar-containing or not, natural or artificial, will trigger at least a small insulin release. If you're avoiding artificial sweeteners, both Zevia and Blue Sky Free sodas are sweetened with erythritol and stevia. I dislike soda in general, but guests have given these sodas the thumbs-up. Oh, and Zevia is now making mixers, including tonic and ginger beer. I quite like their tonic.

ABOUT ALCOHOL

Who says you should never drink alone? Curling up with an adult beverage at the end of the day can make the news more bearable, or inspire you to skip it entirely for something more fun.

No, alcohol does not turn to sugar in the bloodstream. It does, however, stop fat-burning until you burn through it. Keep that in mind.

If you drink, be aware that basic hard liquor has zero carbs, but the panoply of flavored versions—Fireball, Jack Daniel's Honey Whiskey, Captain Morgan, and so on—has sugar added. So stick to the basics. Remember, if it tastes sweet and does not say "sugar-free," it contains sugar.

Be aware that tonic water has as much sugar as soda. Buy sugar-free. If you're avoiding artificial sweeteners, Zevia brand tonic, sweetened with stevia and erythritol, is excellent.

If you're a beer drinker, Michelob Ultra, Corona Premier, Miller Lite, and Milwaukee's Best Light are all quite low in carbs, and Corona Premier is gluten-free, as well.

Dry wines run 1 to 4 grams of carbs per glass—Cabernet, Shiraz, Malbec, Pinot Grigio, Chardonnay, and Chablis are all dry. If you're not sure, ask the wine expert at a good liquor store, or a friend who pays more attention to wine than you do.

Combinations I like: The classic gin and tonic, of course. Tequila with lime juice, orange-flavored stevia, and lime sparkling water, or tequila with lemon-flavored stevia and orange, cranberry-lime, or grapefruit sparkling water. The Lemon Fizz on page 152 is highly refreshing, as well. I confess to not being a big fan of whisky or rum, but if you are, go for it! Whisky and sugar-free ginger ale is a classic combination—Zevia Ginger Beer is quite good.

Here are some other drinkables, ranging from thirst-quenching and refreshing to "filling meal in a glass."

YANKEE GIRL'S ATTEMPT AT SWEET TEA

4 tea bags

1 quart (1 L) boiling water

1 pinch of baking soda

Liquid stevia, monk fruit, or sucralose to equal ⅓ cup (66 g) sugar in sweetness

Ice

I'm an unapologetic Yankee and like my iced tea plain, but I know that sweet tea is considered essential in the South. The baking soda neutralizes tannic acid, creating a particularly smooth tea. If you like lemon in your tea, consider using lemon drop stevia from Sweetleaf.

1. Tie the strings of your tea bags together with a simple overhand knot, to facilitate removal. Put them in a heat-tolerant pitcher, along with the baking soda and sweetener.

2. Pour the boiling water over the tea bags and let them steep for 10 minutes or so.

3. Carefully fish them out with a tongs, let your tea cool, then chill.

4. I don't have to remind you to pour it over ice, do I?

....

4 SERVINGS, each with: 5 Calories; 0 g Fat (0.0% calories from fat); Trace Protein; 1 g Carbohydrate; Trace Dietary Fiber; 1 g Net Carbs

HIBISCUS TEA

I'm on a mission to get more Americans to drink hibiscus tea! It is hugely popular all over the Caribbean. Not only is hibiscus tea low-carb, deliciously fruity, and gorgeous to look at, it is a great source of antioxidants.

Hibiscus tea is also believed to lower blood pressure and blood sugar, lower blood fats, and facilitate weight loss. From an article in the journal *Food & Function*: ". . .consumption of HSE (hibiscus) reduced obesity, abdominal fat, serum FFA (free fatty acids) and improved liver steatosis (fatty liver). HSE could act as an adjuvant for preventing obesity and nonalcoholic fatty liver." All that, and it's deliciously refreshing, too!

However, there are animal studies and traditional herbal pharmacopoeias suggesting that hibiscus may reduce fertility, induce menstruation, and even possibly cause miscarriage. If you're pregnant or trying to be, skip it.

I can get dried hibiscus flowers in bulk at Sahara Mart, my local health/international/gourmet grocery, and at Bloomingfoods, my local health food co-op. If you are not so blessed, the Internet is your friend. I like Mountain Rose Herbs (www.mountainroseherbs.com). Having recently acquired a home carbonation unit, I like to add a splash of strong hibiscus tea to a tall glass of sparkling water.

½ cup (25 g) dried hibiscus flowers

6 cups (1.5 L) boiling water

Ice

Sweetener

1. You know how to make tea, right? Put the dried hibiscus flowers in a heat-proof container and pour in the boiling water. Let it cool, then chill. You can strain it if you like, but I find the flowers stay at the bottom of the container, making pouring clear tea easy.

2. Serve over ice with the sweetener of your choice. A squeeze of lemon or lime might be nice, and consider using lemon- or orange-flavored stevia!

....

4 SERVINGS, each with: 3 Calories; Trace Fat (1.6% calories from fat); Trace Protein; 1 g Carbohydrate; Trace Dietary Fiber; 1 g Net Carbs

COFFEE ALMOND FLOAT

1 cup brewed coffee, chilled (bottled cold brew works well)

¾ cup (175 ml) canned coconut milk

2 teaspoons (3.5 g) cocoa powder

¼ teaspoon almond extract

18 drops dark chocolate–flavored liquid stevia

12 fluid ounces (355 ml) diet cream soda, chilled (I use Zevia)

¼ cup (60 ml) heavy cream, chilled and whipped

How idyllic is this on a hot summer morning? Whip your cream the night before, use bottled cold-brew, and the whole thing will take only a minute or two. I've called this two servings because Zevia cream soda comes in cans, not bottles, and I didn't have a way to preserve the bubbles in the remainder. But if your diet cream soda comes with a screw-on lid, have the second serving the next day.

1. Combine the coffee, coconut milk, cocoa powder, almond extract, and liquid stevia in the blender. Run for a few seconds until combined.

2. Pour into glasses, then pour in the chilled cream soda.

3. Top with the whipped cream and you're done!

....

2 SERVINGS, each with: 276 Calories; 29 g Fat (89.9% calories from fat); 3 g Protein; 5 g Carbohydrate; 1 g Dietary Fiber; 4 g Net Carbs

BREAKFAST COCOA

Why is this breakfast cocoa? Because it has enough protein to serve as breakfast all by itself. But, hey, have it for supper if you like. After a hard day, you can skip cooking a full dinner. Just curl up with this cocoa and a trashy novel. Should you happen to have any whipped cream on hand, you could add a dollop, but it's not essential.

1. Put a small saucepan over medium-low heat and add all the ingredients. Whisk until the cocoa dissolves.

2. Heat through. Done!

....

1 SERVING with: 367 Calories; 28 g Fat (65.5% calories from fat); 25 g Protein; 9 g Carbohydrate; 3 g Dietary Fiber; 6 g Net Carbs

Note: *For a streamlined morning, try this: Put everything through the blender and pour it into a mug. Refrigerate overnight. In the morning, pop it in the microwave for 1 minute, stir, and give it another minute or so, until hot. Or just drink it cold—chocolate milk!*

½ cup (120 ml) canned coconut milk

½ cup (120 ml) unsweetened pourable coconut milk

1 tablespoon (5 g) unsweetened cocoa powder

Liquid stevia, monk fruit, or sucralose to equal 1 tablespoon (13 g) sugar in sweetness (chocolate- or vanilla-flavored stevia is good here)

2 tablespoons (16 g) vanilla whey protein powder (or chocolate whey protein, if you have it)

1 tiny pinch salt

MOCHA MORNING BLAST

½ cup (120 ml) canned coconut milk, chilled

¼ cup (60 ml) unsweetened pourable coconut milk, chilled

¼ avocado, ripe, chilled

1 tablespoon (5 g) cocoa powder

1 tablespoon (8 g) vanilla whey protein powder

1 teaspoon instant coffee

18 drops chocolate-flavored liquid stevia

9 drops vanilla-flavored liquid stevia

This smoothie has it all! Protein to build and repair, plenty of ketogenic fats, great flavor, antioxidants, and your morning caffeine boost, all in one glass! And it tastes like a super-rich milk shake. If you have just chocolate or vanilla stevia, no worries. Use what you've got. The carb count is a little higher here than most recipes in the book, largely because of that avocado. Fear not. Every keto doctor I know says avocados are our very good friends.

Put it all in the blender. Run the blender, scraping the sides once or twice to make sure your cocoa powder and coffee crystals aren't sticking there, until you've got a super-thick, smooth shake. Pour into a car cup and hit the streets. Dare yourself to feel deprived!

....

1 SERVING with: 382 Calories; 34 g Fat (74.6% calories from fat); 15 g Protein; 11 g Carbohydrate; 3 g Dietary Fiber; 8 g Net Carbs

GINGERBREAD COFFEE

2 tablespoons (10 g) ground coffee

¼ teaspoon ground ginger

¼ teaspoon ground cinnamon

1 pinch of ground cloves

1½ cups (355 ml) boiling water

¼ cup (60 ml) canned coconut milk

24 drops English toffee–flavored liquid stevia, or to taste

A great way to start a cold winter morning! If you'd like a little protein, too, whisk in a tablespoon or two of vanilla whey protein powder.

1. If you're not using a Keurig—I haven't bothered buying one—combine the coffee with the spices before brewing, then brew according to your unit, and pour into your mug. If you use a Keurig, make a 10-ounce serving, putting the spices in the cup ahead of time.

2. Stir in the coconut milk and stevia, and it's done!

....

1 SERVING with: 115 Calories; 12 g Fat (88.0% calories from fat); 1 g Protein; 2 g Carbohydrate; Trace Dietary Fiber; 2 g Net Carbs

THE BASIC KETO HIGHBALL

To my mind, the highball—hard liquor plus soda, club soda, or sparkling water—is the best drink for the keto dieter. You could just drink your liquor straight, but you'll go through it faster. Mix it with plenty of zero-carb liquid, and it'll last you through a full episode of *American Horror Story*, and maybe two. Keeps you hydrated and tastes good, too.

1. Grab a good, big glass. Pour in your shot of liquor, half-shot of lime or lemon juice, and the liquid stevia.

2. Fill the glass with ice, then pour in your mixer.

....

1 SERVING with: 68 Calories; Trace Fat (2.3% calories from fat); Trace Protein; 1 g Carbohydrate; Trace Dietary Fiber; 1 Net Carb

1 shot (1½ ounces [45 ml]) vodka, tequila, gin, whisky, or rum (but nothing sweetened!)

½ shot (¾ ounce [22 ml]) lime juice or lemon juice (optional)

12 drops liquid lemon drop or Valencia orange–flavored stevia (optional)

Ice

Chilled sparkling water (your preferred flavor) or sugar-free tonic water to fill

LEMON FIZZ

½ lemon

12 drops liquid lemon drop stevia

1 shot vodka

Ice

Club soda

The whole alcopop phenomenon took hold after I quit eating sugar, so I have never tried Hard Lemonade. But a fizzy, lemony libation sounded good on a hot August evening, so I created this. Feel free to skip the vodka for a refreshing fizzy lemonade.

Feel free to use half a lime instead of half a lemon; with the lemon drop stevia, you'll get a lemon-lime flavor. You could also use Valencia orange–flavored stevia for a lemon-orange flavor.

1. Grate about ¼ teaspoon of lemon zest into a big glass. Squeeze the juice from the lemon half, getting all you can, and add to the glass. Add the lemon drop stevia and the vodka.

2. Fill with ice, then club soda. Done!

....

1 SERVING with: 70 Calories; Trace Fat (5.3% calories from fat); Trace Protein; 3 g Carbohydrate; Trace Dietary Fiber; 3 g Net Carbs

TROPICAL COOLER

If you're a fan of fruity drinks with umbrellas in 'em, you have to try this! You can skip the tequila if you want a nonalcoholic drink, or you can swap in vodka if you don't like tequila. But it's awfully good this way.

Fill a big ol' glass with ice. Pour the tequila and lime juice over the ice, then add the hibiscus tea and ginger beer. The teeny umbrella is optional.

....

1 SERVING with: 152 Calories; Trace Fat (1.9% calories from fat); 1 g Protein; 6 g Carbohydrate; 1 g Dietary Fiber; 5 g Net Carbs

2 ounces tequila

2 tablespoons (28 ml) lime juice

½ cup (120 ml) Hibiscus Tea (page 143), chilled

½ cup (120 ml) diet ginger beer or ginger ale, chilled (I use Zevia ginger beer)

CHAPTER 8

CONDIMENTS AND SAUCES

Why make sauces and condiments? Because ketchup has 4 grams of carb per tablespoon, and who ever stopped at 1 tablespoon? Because mayonnaise is a Festival of Bad Oils, even if it says "made with olive oil" (the word "with" is the tip-off), while homemade mayonnaise can be one of your best sources of highly ketogenic fats. The same can be said for salad dressings. Because sauces and condiments can enhance simple meat, poultry, fish, seafoods, eggs, and steamed or roasted vegetables endlessly.

Sauces are also a great way to add fat to low-fat foods like fish and seafood, chicken, and vegetables.

I've skipped the obvious, here: Lemon butter can be used to great effect on everything from fish and seafood to asparagus and broccoli. (I swear, lemon butter is the reason I loved broccoli even as a tiny child.)

EASY NO-SUGAR-ADDED KETCHUP

Heinz no-sugar-added ketchup is quite good, but it's pricier and includes artificial sweeteners some people avoid. This is a cinch, tastes great, and has no artificial sweeteners.

Combine everything in a nonreactive (stainless steel, ceramic nonstick, or enamelware) saucepan and bring to a simmer. Let it cook for 15 minutes, let it cool, and it's done. I used a funnel to pour mine into an old squeeze-type ketchup bottle for ease of use, but a jar or snap-top container will do just fine. Stored in the refrigerator, it will keep indefinitely.

....

24 SERVINGS of 1 tablespoon (15 ml) each, with: 6 Calories; Trace Fat (3.5% calories from fat); Trace Protein; 2 g Carbohydrate; Trace Dietary Fiber; 2 g Net Carbs

1 (15-ounce [425 g]) can tomato sauce

½ cup (120 ml) cider vinegar

3 tablespoons (45 g) erythritol blend (see page 14)

1 teaspoon salt

½ teaspoon onion powder

¼ teaspoon garlic powder

MCT MAYO

1 egg

1 egg yolk

1 tablespoon (15 ml) lemon juice

1 tablespoon (15 ml) red wine vinegar

1 teaspoon dry mustard

¼ teaspoon salt

2 drops stevia (optional)

1 cup (235 ml) MCT oil
(see page 16)

Why are you making your own mayonnaise? Not just to avoid the soy oil in commercially made mayonnaise, but to create a great way to get more highly ketogenic MCT oil into your diet. Every time I make tuna or chicken salad with this mayonnaise, I test in deep ketosis later in the day.

This is more flavorful than grocery store mayo; you can halve the lemon juice, vinegar, and mustard if you want it milder.

If you're worried about raw eggs, you can pasteurize 'em; see the note below. I just use raw ones, and I never get food poisoning, but your risks are your own to take.

1. Combine the egg, egg yolk, lemon juice, vinegar, mustard, salt, and stevia, if using, in your blender or food processor. Have the oil standing by in a measuring cup with a pouring lip.

2. Turn on the blender or food processor and let it run for 15 seconds or so. Leave it running and pour in the oil, in a slow, steady stream about the diameter of a pencil lead. Don't pour too fast!

3. When all the oil is in, it's mayonnaise. Put it in a jar and stick it in the fridge, where it will keep for about 1 week.

....

8 SERVINGS of 2 tablespoons (30 g) each, with: 258 Calories; 28 g Fat (97.7% calories from fat); 1 g Protein; Trace Carbohydrate; Trace Dietary Fiber; 0 g Net Carbs

Note: *Many people are terrified of raw eggs, having been convinced by officialdom that they're salmonella bombs. This is overblown hysteria; fewer than 1 in 20,000 uncracked, properly refrigerated eggs is contaminated. But if you are worried—when making mayonnaise, say, or Caesar salad dressing —you can pasteurize your eggs.*

To pasteurize raw eggs: *Put the eggs in a saucepan and cover with water. Put the saucepan over high heat and bring the water to 140°F (66°C) degrees (you'll need an instant-read thermometer). Maintain them at that temperature—and no hotter, or else you'll cook them—for 3 minutes. Then immediately pour off the hot water, and rinse the eggs with several changes of cold water. Store in the refrigerator until needed, or use right away.*

VARIABLE VINAIGRETTE

If you've been buying bottled salad dressing, you may not realize just how simple it is to make. Why make your own? Because virtually all bottled salad dressings contain bad oils, and many have sugar. This will take you all of 3 minutes.

½ cup (120 ml) extra virgin olive oil

2 teaspoons minced garlic

¼ cup (60 ml) vinegar (see suggestions in step 2)

2 teaspoons Dijon mustard

Scant ¼ teaspoon salt

⅛ teaspoon pepper

1. Put everything in a clean old jar, lid it tightly, and shake. Done! Store in the fridge and shake again before using, natch.

2. Now for the "variable" part. Try:

- Red wine vinegar plus a few pinches of dried oregano—good with Italian and Greek foods.
- White wine vinegar—good with milder-flavored greens, or on fish or chicken. Try adding a pinch of dried tarragon.
- Balsamic vinegar—gives a slight sweetness, especially good if you're having your salad with a steak. A couple of teaspoons of grated Parmesan tastes great here.
- White balsamic vinegar is milder than the darker version. Use with tender greens like butter lettuce.
- Apple cider vinegar—I grew up on apple cider vinaigrette! Try this with a few drops of English toffee–flavored stevia, a drop or two of maple extract, and 1 tablespoon (13 g) of bacon grease swapped for 1 tablespoon (28 ml) of oil.
- If you find extra virgin olive oil too strong, use half MCT oil (see page 16). Not only is it bland, it is highly ketogenic.
- For a creamy dressing, swap 2 tablespoons (30 g) of MCT Mayo (page 156) or sour cream for 2 tablespoons (28 ml) of the oil.
- For the original form of blue cheese dressing, add 1 to 2 tablespoons (8 to 16 g) of crumbled blue cheese to the basic red wine vinaigrette.
- For a creamy blue cheese dressing, use 2 tablespoons (30 g) MCT mayo and 1 to 2 tablespoons (15 to 30 g) of sour cream in place of some of the oil. Add 1 to 2 tablespoons (8 to 16 g) crumbled blue cheese, and a dash of Worcestershire.

4 SERVINGS of the basic recipe, each with: 245 Calories; 27 g Fat (97.2% calories from fat); Trace Protein; 2 g Carbohydrate; Trace Dietary Fiber; 2 g Net Carbs

CAESAR SALAD DRESSING

½ teaspoon minced garlic

1 anchovy fillet

1 tablespoon (15 ml) lemon juice

½ teaspoon Dijon or brown mustard

½ teaspoon Worcestershire sauce

½ cup (118 g) MCT Mayo (page 156)

¼ cup (25 g) grated Parmesan cheese

Traditional Caesar salad dressing is made fresh and includes a coddled egg. It occurred to me that, being egg-thickened, mayonnaise might be doctored into a quicker, easier version. Voila!

Combine all the ingredients in your compact food processor and run it until the garlic and anchovy are pulverized. That's it! Put one-third of it on your current salad, and scrape the rest into a small jar or snap-top container, refrigerate, and use the remainder the next day.

....

3 SERVINGS of about 3 tablespoons (45 ml), each with: 299 Calories; 33 g Fat (94.1% calories from fat); 4 g Protein; 1 g Carbohydrate; Trace Dietary Fiber; 1 g Net Carbs

HOLLANDAISE FOR CHEATERS

1 tablespoon (14 g) butter

¼ cup (60 g) MCT Mayo (page 156)

2 tablespoons (30 g) sour cream

1½ teaspoons lemon juice

½ teaspoon Dijon or brown mustard

⅛ teaspoon paprika

1 dash hot sauce (Louisiana, Frank's, or Tabasco)

Not cheating on your diet, just cheating on the traditional hollandaise recipe. Let's face it, you're not going to make hollandaise just for yourself. But you might like to have something to top asparagus or poached eggs, right?

1. In a small, nonreactive saucepan—stainless steel, enamel, ceramic nonstick, or the like—over very low heat, melt the butter.

2. Add the mayo, sour cream, lemon juice, mustard, paprika, and hot sauce, and whisk together. Keep whisking until it's just warmed through—do not let it boil! Disaster will result. Just warm it. Store extra in the refrigerator in an airtight container for up to 1 week.

....

2 SERVINGS, each with: 342 Calories; 37 g Fat (96.3% calories from fat); 2 g Protein; 2 g Carbohydrate; Trace Dietary Fiber; 2 g Net Carbs

CHEESE SAUCE

You can use this to make shirataki mac-and-cheese, of course, but how about pouring it over broccoli? Cauliflower? It is good with all the usual cheese sauce suspects. You can also stir it into pureed cauliflower, also known as "fauxtatoes," now available in your grocery store's freezer case.

¼ cup (60 ml) heavy cream

¼ cup (28 g) shredded Cheddar cheese

1 tablespoon (6 g) whipped cream cheese

¼ teaspoon brown mustard

Salt and pepper

1. Have all the ingredients measured and on hand before you start. Pour the heavy cream into a small saucepan and put it over medium-low heat. Whisk the cream as it heats. When it's hot, add the cheese a little at a time, whisking each addition until it melts, then adding more.

2. Whisk in the cream cheese. When it's melted, stir in the mustard and salt and pepper to taste, and you're done.

....

1 SERVING with: 355 Calories; 35 g Fat (87.4% calories from fat); 9 g Protein; 3 g Carbohydrate; Trace Dietary Fiber; 3 g Net Carbs

ALFREDO SAUCE

¼ cup (60 ml) heavy cream

¼ teaspoon minced garlic

¼ cup (20 g) shredded Parmesan cheese

1 tablespoon (6 g) whipped cream cheese

Salt and pepper

The great thing about making a cream sauce for one is that because of the small volume, it cooks very quickly. You can have this done in the time it takes to microwave your shirataki noodles! Another great use: Sauté diced chicken breast, a little onion, and some thawed "cut" broccoli, then stir in this sauce and top with a little extra Parmesan. Yum.

1. Have all the ingredients measured and on hand before you start. Pour the heavy cream into a small saucepan and put it over medium-low heat. Add the garlic and whisk the cream as it heats.

2. When the cream is hot, add the cheese, a little at a time, whisking each addition until it melts, then adding more.

3. Whisk in the cream cheese. When it melts, add salt and pepper to taste, and you're done.

....

1 SERVING with: 324 Calories; 31 g Fat (85.0% calories from fat); 9 g Protein; 3 g Carbohydrate; Trace Dietary Fiber; 3 g Net Carbs

BEARNAISE BUTTER

Four servings?! Yes, four servings. It'll keep fine covered in the fridge. You can whip it out whenever you have a steak, scoop out a tablespoonful, and feel sinfully indulgent yet oddly virtuous.

1. In a small, nonreactive saucepan—stainless steel, enamelware, ceramic nonstick, or the like—over low heat, combine the vinegar and shallot. Crumble the tarragon between your fingers as you add it, to release the flavor. Let it simmer until the vinegar reduces to a bare film on the bottom of the pan.

2. Add the butter, melt, and stir. That's it! Stash in a snap-top container in the refrigerator for at least 1 week and use the next time you're having a steak.

....

4 SERVINGS, each with: 106 Calories; 12 g Fat (95.1% calories from fat); Trace Protein; 1 g Carbohydrate; Trace Dietary Fiber; 1g Net Carbs

2 tablespoons (28 ml) tarragon vinegar or white wine vinegar

1 tablespoon minced shallot

1 teaspoon dried tarragon

¼ cup (55 g) butter

EXTRA SPECIAL SAUCE

If I've ever eaten a Big Mac, it was so long ago that I've forgotten it, so I can't tell you if this is a clone of McD's Special Sauce. But it sure dresses up a burger. The lettuce, cheese, pickles, and onions are up to you.

Just stir everything together. Done! If you're only making one burger immediately, store the leftovers in a snap-top container in the fridge and have another burger later in the week.

....

2 SERVINGS, each with: 102 Calories; 12 g Fat (96.9% calories from fat); Trace Protein; 1 g Carbohydrate; Trace Dietary Fiber; 1 g Net Carbs

2 tablespoons (30 g) MCT Mayo (page 156)

1 tablespoon (10 g) chopped Sugar-Free Bread and Butter Pickles, plus ½ teaspoon pickle brine (page 167)

1 teaspoon no-sugar-added ketchup, homemade (page 155) or store-bought

½ teaspoon yellow mustard

1 teaspoon white balsamic vinegar

Liquid stevia, monk fruit, or sucralose to equal ¼ teaspoon sugar in sweetness

1 pinch of paprika

1 pinch of onion powder

1 pinch of garlic powder

HORSERADISH BUTTER

2 tablespoons (28 g) butter, softened

1 tablespoon (15 g) prepared horseradish

½ teaspoon minced garlic

½ teaspoon lemon juice

Great for burgers or steaks. Or over fish, or melted, to dip seafood in. I mean, butter, horseradish, garlic, and lemon juice. How far wrong can you go?

Combine everything in a small food processor and run until well-blended, or you can just mash it all together with a fork, if you prefer. By the way, the food processor is the reason I made two servings' worth—one serving would barely be enough to reach the blades. Store any extra in a snap-top container in the refrigerator for 1 to 2 weeks. If you want to halve this, blend it by hand.

....

2 SERVINGS, each with: 107 Calories; 12 g Fat (94.7% calories from fat); Trace Protein; 1 g Carbohydrate; Trace Dietary Fiber; 1 g Net Carbs

HORSERADISH-MUSTARD SAUCE, DIP, MARINADE, AND DRESSING

You can mix this up in a minute or two, and the uses are many. It's great on chicken salad, as a sauce or marinade for beef or pork steaks, or over fish fillets. Great for dipping vegetables, too. Really, it goes anywhere you want a hit of flavor and fat.

Combine everything in a bowl and stir it up. It's nice to refrigerate this for a few hours before using, to let the flavors marry, but hardly essential. Store any extra in a snap-top container in the refrigerator for up to 1 week.

....

2 SERVINGS, each with: 133 Calories; 15 g Fat (94.5% calories from fat); 1 g Protein; 1 g Carbohydrate; Trace Dietary Fiber; 1 g Net Carbs

2 tablespoons (30 g) MCT Mayo (page 156)

2 tablespoons (30 g) sour cream

1 teaspoon prepared horseradish

1 teaspoon Dijon or brown mustard

1 teaspoon cider vinegar

1 pinch of salt

PEANUT SAUCE

½ cup (120 ml) canned coconut milk

¼ cup (65 g) natural peanut butter (I use smooth)

1 teaspoon minced garlic

1 tablespoon soy sauce

1 teaspoon fish sauce

1 teaspoon lemon juice

½ teaspoon dark sesame oil

¼ teaspoon dried red pepper flakes

4 drops English toffee–flavored liquid stevia

Many peanut sauce recipes call for equal quantities of coconut milk and peanut butter. But since coconut milk is lower in carbs and higher in fat than peanut butter, I shifted the ratios—and still came up with a yummy sauce! Why make six servings? Because I needed sufficient ingredients to engage with the blades of my compact food processor. This keeps for a few days in the fridge, so just use it up later in the week.

Nothing complicated here. Just combine all the ingredients in a compact food processor, and process until you have a smooth, consistent paste. Store in an airtight container in the refrigerator for up to 5 days.

....
6 SERVINGS, each with: 106 Calories; 9 g Fat (77.4% calories from fat); 3 g Protein; 3 g Carbohydrate; 1 g Dietary Fiber; 2 g Net Carbs

SHORTCUT TARTAR SAUCE

Great with any fish or seafood, or in place of the orange sauce on the crab cakes, page 110. Handy hint: One or two dill pickle hamburger chips and a really small scallion—or a little scallion from the salad bar—help you make this with no awkward leftover bits.

Measure out your mayo into a small dish and add the pickle, capers, scallion, and parsley. Add the lemon juice and stir it all up. Add salt and pepper to taste and bring on the fish! Store in an airtight container in the fridge for up to 1 week.

....

2 SERVINGS, each with: 199 Calories; 23 g Fat (98.6% calories from fat); Trace Protein; Trace Carbohydrate; Trace Dietary Fiber; 0 g Net Carbs

¼ cup (60 g) MCT Mayo (page 156)

1 teaspoon chopped dill pickle

1 teaspoon capers, drained and minced

1 teaspoon minced scallion

1 teaspoon minced fresh parsley

1 teaspoon lemon juice

Salt and pepper

CHIPOTLE CREMA

I made this to go on the Southwestern Tuna on Avocado (page 73), then realized it would be useful in many other ways. Try it on chicken, fish, a cheese-and-avocado omelet, over a steak, as a dip for cucumber slices—all sorts of ways!

Combine everything in a small dish and use a fork to stir it up and mash the chipotle. That's it!

....

1 SERVING with: 100 Calories; 9 g Fat (79.7% calories from fat); 2 g Protein; 3 g Carbohydrate; 1 g Dietary Fiber; 2 g Net Carbs

3 tablespoons (45 g) sour cream

1 tablespoon (15 ml) unsweetened pourable coconut milk

1 tablespoon (15 ml) lime juice

½ chipotle chile canned in adobo, plus ¼ teaspoon adobo sauce

Salt

SALAMI SPREAD OR PASTE

4 ounces (115 g) salami

¼ cup (60 ml) olive oil

2 Calabrian peppers packed in oil

1 teaspoon sun-dried tomato pesto

OMG. So easy, so versatile, so good! Toss it with a little olive oil and Parmesan, with shirataki or zoodles, add it to a mozzarella or provolone omelet, mix it with whipped cream cheese and Parmesan for an easy dip or to stuff mushrooms or into a chicken breast—use your imagination!

The salami is the important thing here. Do not buy the cheap stuff! Sopressata is good, but any really high-quality salami should serve.

The sun-dried tomato pesto is optional, but good. I know, I know, you're left with the rest of the jar. My jar is over a year old and still going strong. If you have a full-sized fridge, it's a worthwhile investment. If you can't get the pesto, use one sun-dried tomato half.

Regarding those Calabrian peppers: I got mine at Kroger in Bloomington, Indiana, so how hard can they be to find?

Put everything in a compact food processor and run until you have a paste. That's it! Store in a snap-top container in the refrigerator for up to 1 week.

....

4 SERVINGS, each with: 211 Calories; 20 g Fat (82.3% calories from fat); 5 g Protein; 5 g Carbohydrate; 1 g Dietary Fiber; 4 g Net Carbs

SUGAR-FREE BREAD AND BUTTER PICKLES

I've used sugar-free bread-and-butter pickles in a few recipes in this book, and they're a must in tuna salad as far as I'm concerned. Sugar-free sweet pickles are available in grocery stores, but they all contain artificial sweeteners, and I know some of you avoid them. Here's a quick-and-easy way to make your own. This yields a pickle that is a bit less sweet than commercially made bread and butter pickles. I prefer them this way, but you certainly can add more sweetener, if you like.

Drain the liquid from your jar of pickles into a nonreactive saucepan, leaving the pickles in the jar. Add the sweetener, allspice, celery seeds, mustard seeds, and cloves and bring to a simmer. Let it cook for a few minutes to allow the flavors blend, then let it cool for just a minute or two before pouring the seasoned brine back into the jar. Put the lid on and stash in the fridge. Let 'em marinate for at least a few days before using, then use like any sweet pickles.

....

32 SERVINGS, each with: 6 Calories; Trace Fat (14.3% calories from fat); Trace Protein; 1 g Carbohydrate; Trace Dietary Fiber; 1 g Net Carbs

1 (32-ounce [905 g]) jar sour pickles or dill spears

Liquid stevia or monk fruit to equal 1 cup (200 g) sugar in sweetness

½ teaspoon ground allspice

½ teaspoon celery seeds

1½ teaspoons mustard seeds

3 to 4 whole cloves

RESOURCES

SPECIALTY PRODUCTS

Amazon.com, unsurprisingly, has a staggering array of products that work for us, from sugar-free sweeteners to shirataki noodles.

Netrition.com specializes in nutritional products and has a good low carb products section.

That said, make an exploratory mission to local grocery stores some day when you have a little time, just to see what they have that works for a keto diet.

Also, remember that most health food stores are wonderful about special-ordering things. I special order everything—from shirataki noodles to 4-pound (1.8 kg) jars of plain gelatin to my beloved Spike Vege-Sal in the big box—from Sahara Mart and Bloomingfoods, our two fantastic local health food stores. No shipping charge!

PODCASTS

I confess to not having been bitten by the podcast bug, but here are a couple of lists of keto podcasts others have thought well of:

perfectketo.com/best-keto-podcasts-2018

thelowcarbleader.com/category/best-low-carb -leader-podcasts

INFORMATION

dietdoctor.com

carbsmart.com

healclinics.com/articles

healclinics.com/low-carb-myths

If, like me, you are a geek, you can access medical research abstracts and sometimes full articles at **pubmed.com**. Search "ketogenic" or "ketones" and whatever else you're interested in—ketogenic Alzheimer's, ketogenic cancer, ketogenic diabetic nephropathy, and the like.

(Full disclosure: I am involved with both HEAL and CarbSmart.)

SUPPORT

There are hundreds of low carb/keto support groups online, especially on Facebook. I cannot list them all here! I recommend that you find one or two whose culture you enjoy and hang out. This is especially vital if you do not have support at home. On Facebook I am Dana Carpender's Hold the Toast Press. I also participate in some others, including HEALCare For Life, Old School Low Carb, Low Carb Ladybug, and I Love Low Carb.

INDEX

ACKNOWLEDGMENTS

Thank you to Jill Alexander, Renae Haines, John Gettings, Nyle Vialet, and Heather Godin—and anyone else at Fair Winds I'm spacing out on—for dealing with my occasional flakiness.

And, always and forever, thank you to Eric, That Nice Boy I Married. He makes more runs to the grocery store than I do, fixes my computer by merely glaring at it, offers me honest feedback on recipes, conveniently enjoys some foods I do not, and is just plain nice to have around the house.

ABOUT THE AUTHOR

Among Dana Carpender's earliest memories are decorating Christmas cookies as only a three-year-old can and making gravy while so young she needed a step stool to reach the stove. She simply cannot remember not cooking.

When, at age nineteen, she realized that ditching a serious sugar addiction (plus dropping refined flour) improved her mood and energy, she had to learn to cook again. But by her mid-thirties, a low-fat diet rich in "good carbs" was not working. "I whole-grain-and-beaned my way up to a size 20 with high blood pressure," she says.

A nutrition book from 1952 reminded her that in her youth everyone knew that if you wanted to lose weight you gave up potatoes, spaghetti, bread, and sweets. She slashed the carbs from her diet. Within three days, her clothes were loose and her energy level and mood had sky-rocketed. There was no going back.

Only one problem: She had to ditch all her low-fat, grain-full recipes. Severe kitchen disorientation was the result. "One night I walked into the kitchen and had no idea what to cook for supper. It made me angry. I vowed I would learn to cook this new way as well as I had the old way." Thus was a new career born.

"Naysayers have told me all along that this way of eating would wreck my health," she says. "It's now been more than 23 years—38% of my life—and I am still stubbornly alive and well. And I still enjoy this food!"

Dana lives in Bloomington, Indiana with her husband Eric Schmitz, often referred to in her work as That Nice Boy I Married; and two dogs, a cat, and an indeterminate number of chickens, who supply her with glorious, fresh eggs.